ARCHITECTURAL DRAWINGS

Hidden Masterpieces from Sir John Soane's Museum

ARCHITECTURAL DRAWINGS

Hidden Masterpieces from Sir John Soane's Museum

Frances Sands

BATSFORD

Contents

After Federico Zuccaro, study of wall decoration, a pope receiving homage in Rome, from the *Margaret Chinnery Album*, sixteenth century, SM volume 114/9. Photograph: Ardon Bar-Hama.

Office of Sir John Soane, RA lecture drawing, the Ionic orders set in a landscape, as designed by the Ten Masters in *Fréart's Parallèle*, 1806–19, SM 23/5/2. Photograph: Ardon Bar-Hama.

PALLADIO   SCAMOZZI

SERLIO   VIGNOLA   D. BARBARO   CATANEO   L. B. ALBERTI   VIOLA   I. BULLANT   P. DE LORME

Foreword

In the very first of his Royal Academy Lectures as Professor of Architecture, John Soane stressed the importance of drawing as an essential attribute for the young architect, together with a mastery of mathematics, geometry and hydraulics. Indeed, Soane's own instruction under Thomas Sandby and George Dance reinforced the centrality of drawing as a means of expressing new ideas and mastering the intricacies of the great architectural traditions of the past, and such ideas formed the basis of his collections, both of architectural drawings and of plaster casts replicating the elements of architecture to scale.

As Soane's collecting habits grew and matured, his interests broadened to include a conspectus of building styles, and the 30,000 architectural drawings in the possession of his museum constitute the greater part of his legacy to the nation. Scholars and students still come to Lincoln's Inn Fields to learn and be inspired by his collection, and it is our hope that this book will give a flavour of that legacy to those unable to visit Sir John Soane's Museum. I am grateful to Dr Frances Sands, Curator of Drawings and Books, and to all my curatorial colleagues for their efforts in the production of such a handsome and scholarly book, one in which John Soane himself would have taken great pleasure and pride.

Bruce Boucher, Deborah Loeb Brice Director
Sir John Soane's Museum   December 2019

——• Office of Sir John Soane, RA lecture drawing, Sir William Chambers's House of Confucius at Kew Gardens, Richmond, 1806–19, SM 17/5/9. Photograph: Geremy Butler.

Introduction

A visit to Sir John Soane's Museum in Lincoln's Inn Fields is surely one of the great cultural and aesthetic pleasures in life, and certainly an essential item on any London tourist's itinerary. The creation of Sir John Soane (1753–1837), one of Britain's finest architects, collectors and teachers, in this museum we find the extraordinary survival of a private Georgian house-museum-turned-national-collection.

Born in 1753 in Goring-on-Thames in Oxfordshire, John Soan (later Soane) was the son of a bricklayer. The loss of his father in 1767, when Soane was only 14 years old, prompted his removal from Baker's School in Reading, upon which he followed in his father and older brother's footsteps and began a career as a bricklayer. Most fortunately for the young Soane, while working as a bricklayer in 1768, an architect's assistant and family acquaintance, James Peacock, noticed Soane's talents as a draughtsman and arranged for him to enter into an architectural apprenticeship in the office of the much-admired George Dance the Younger (1741–1825). Three years later, aged 18, Soane was accepted as a student of architecture at the RA, affording him access to their library, lecture series and, most importantly of all, entitling him to submit one of his own drawings to the architecture category of the RA annual competition. In 1776, when Soane was only 23 years old, he won the RA gold medal for architecture with a design for a monumental bridge to cross the River Thames. His success at the RA enabled Soane – through the good offices of Sir William Chambers (1722–96) – to meet King George III and resulted in his nomination for a travelling studentship. This was a scholarship for three years, funded by a royal pension and worth £60 per annum plus expenses of £30 each way; the idea being that the recipient should use the money to undertake a Grand Tour of Europe for the benefit of their education. In 1778 Soane travelled via France to Italy where he busied himself

in acquiring a thorough knowledge of the classical tradition of architecture, making drawings of the antique ruins that he encountered and forging contacts with other British grand tourists who would later become his patrons. The importance of Soane's Grand Tour to his development as an architect was never lost on him, and he noted the date of 18 March in his diary – the day he had ventured forth in 1778 – almost every year for the rest of his life.

Unfortunately, many of Soane's Grand Tour drawings were lost along with other possessions when the bottom of his trunk fell out as he crossed the Alps on his way home. Among his few surviving souvenirs were a handful of drawings by Italian draughtsmen and four engravings from Giovanni Battista Piranesi's *Vedute di Roma* (1748–78), which had been given to him by that great man himself. When Soane returned to London from his Grand Tour in 1780, he set about establishing his own architectural practice and quickly achieved a handful of commissions thanks partly to the many connections he had made abroad and partly to his innovative pared-down Neo-classical style. His first major success came in 1788 when he was appointed Architect to the Bank of England in the face of considerable competition.

In 1790, Soane's wife Eliza received a major inheritance from her uncle, George Wyatt, a London property developer, enabling the couple to purchase and rebuild the first of three houses on the north side of Lincoln's Inn Fields. Numbers 12, 13 and 14 now make up Sir John Soane's Museum. The houses were acquired sequentially in 1792, 1807 and 1823, as Soane required additional space for his growing collection of artworks, antiquities, furniture, books and drawings, which had largely been purchased in the London sale rooms. Soane first resided at number 12 Lincoln's Inn Fields, and later at number 13 where he developed his museum in place of former stables across the back of the houses. It was this building and

the collection it contains that Soane left to the British nation with a private Act of Parliament, passed in 1833, and requiring that the museum be kept as far as possible as it was at the time of Soane's death. He died four years later in 1837 when he was just shy of 84 years old.

It is both wonderful and rather sad that Soane left his house-museum to the British nation. He and Eliza had two sons who survived past infancy, John junior and George, whom Soane had hoped would follow him into the architectural profession and create a Soane-family dynasty much like the Dances or the Adams, but this was not to be the case. The older boy, John junior, died from tuberculosis aged only 37 in 1823, and his younger brother, George, was hot tempered and fiscally profligate. After Soane had refused to bail George out of debtors' prison in 1815, George sought revenge on his father and wrote two articles in *The Champion* newspaper in which he was heavily critical of his father's work:

> In the Bank of England, the greater part of which is built by Mr SOANE, *we meet with the remnants of mausoleums, caryatids, pillars from temples, ornaments from the Pantheon, and all heaped together with a perversion of taste that is truly admirable. He steals a bit here, and a bit there, and in piling up these collected thefts, he imagines he has done his duty and earned the honours of an artist. Depraved as is the present taste, such follies will not pass for wisdom; the public laugh at these extravagances, which are too dull for madness, and too mad for the soberness of reason.*

On discovering that the author of such poisonous words was his own son, the enraged Soane felt utterly betrayed by George, but worse still was Eliza's reaction. Already suffering with gallstones, Eliza described George's words as having delivered her 'death blow'

and she died six weeks later on 22 November 1815. With Eliza's death, Soane lost his closest friend and confidante. He felt that it had been precipitated by George's insults, and so framed the two articles adorned with a plaque reading 'Death Blows', and George was disinherited. While this story of betrayal and loss is dramatic, the most important things to remember about Soane are his professional and pedagogical successes. He left his museum as an 'Academy of Architecture' for the benefit of both students and scholars of architecture, painting and sculpture as well as the public, and his drawings collection constitutes a crucial element of that purpose.

At one time, Soane had considered specifically creating a Gallery for Drawings and Prints, but instead he built a space in which varied media of art could be displayed together, with framed drawings included within the domestic and Picture Room spaces. Former Soane Museum Curator Peter Thornton has suggested that Soane was rejecting a more formal, typological and academic arrangement 'in favour of one that he hoped would stimulate the beholder's imagination by subtle suggestion brought about by placing often highly disparate objects in close proximity to each other'. For some modern visitors the *horror vacui* of the Soane Museum's collections of rich and varied artworks can appear as an almost overwhelming maelstrom of objects. Certainly, Soane's arrangements resist an obvious narrative, but many visitors are able to discern an iconographic programme, albeit one that is no less pleasingly intense in the density of its collected whole. Happily, few visitors of the last two centuries have failed to appreciate the beauty and genius of the place. Paintings, sculpture, furniture, books and other objects are arranged together within Soane's home at Lincoln's Inn Fields. The house functioned both as Soane's laboratory of architectural and interior decorative experimentation, but also as a bespoke container for his collections – a *gesamtkunstwerk* – in which the architecture and collection are carefully arranged in harmony with one another as a complete work of art. Soane himself spoke of 'the union and close connexion between Painting, Sculpture and Architecture' in the 1835 *Description of the House and Museum*.

—• Charles James Richardson for Sir John Soane, the Cawdor Vase and Picture Room chimneypiece at 14 Lincoln's Inn Fields, London, 28 September 1825, SM volume 82/16. Photograph: Ardon Bar-Hama.

This allows the viewer's gaze to rove from one extraordinary item to another, and while being extremely therapeutic to the historically and culturally inclined, this is not a place for visual repose!

Among this great and wonderful mêlée of objects one can discern a relatively small number of exquisite framed drawings, grouped within spaces including the Picture Room and the Breakfast Room, alongside many other two- and three-dimensional pieces. Some of these are the work of great and famous hands such as those of Giovanni Battista Piranesi (1720–78), but the majority show Soane's own architectural output, often in the form of drawings by the extraordinarily talented artist and draughtsman Joseph Michael Gandy (1771–1843). However, these framed drawings within the public rooms at the museum are merely the tip of the iceberg, with the vast majority of Soane's drawings collection remaining hidden from sight. Their presence is sometimes hinted at and if one takes a moment to look down at what another object of interest might be resting upon, it is often a cupboard, press or chest filled with drawings. At the end of Soane's life the entire drawings collection was housed within the museum itself, whereas today many sheets are contained in purpose-designed presses created in the 1920s for the non-public areas of the building. As such, the collection is now dispersed across the entire building, in spaces both public and private, and the running of the museum's Research Library is regularly as much a treasure hunt as it is an intellectual feast.

But how do we define a drawing as opposed to any other two-dimensional work of art? The word 'drawing' is applied to an enormous variety of different media and art forms spanning an array of techniques, for example, a charcoal sketch portrait versus a watercolour architectural view. Moreover, how has the concept of a 'drawing' evolved? In fourteenth- to sixteenth-century Italy, during the Renaissance, the word *disegno* described drawing or designing in monochromatic two dimensions. This did not encompass the use of colour, but crucially, it demanded both a skill in draughtsmanship as well as the intellectual capacity for invention and creative design. This raised the artist above the realm of other mere mortals, aligning him or her with God the Creator, and thus the two-dimensional arts were placed, hierarchically, above other crafts.

In the early modern era, the higher notion of invention associated with *disegno* was, to some degree, lost. Drawing was no longer necessarily linked with the creative design process as it became commonplace to copy for pleasure or professional purposes – think of the work of a paid draughtsman. As such, 'drawing' as an art form came to be associated with any artistic output in which drawing instruments such as pencils, pens and brushes were used to make marks on paper or other two-dimensional media like vellum. It is the significance of the drawn line onto which wash or other media can be applied that distinguishes a drawing from a painting. A watercolour drawing will overlay a line drawing, usually in pencil, but when an artist applies watercolour directly to the paper without the guide of any lines, in a more fluid manner, this is generally considered to be a painting. Naturally there are exceptions to this, for example, the use of dots, either drawn on or pricked from one sheet to another, can serve a similar purpose to the drawn line.

By far the largest proportion of Soane's drawings collection consists of architectural drawings as opposed to any other genre, such as drawn portraits or landscapes. There are large groups of architectural drawings by well-known figures such as Nicholas Hawksmoor (*c*.1662–1736) and Sir William Chambers, as well – of course – as a great many drawings from Soane's own architectural office. Soane's acquisition of drawings was piecemeal and skilfully opportunistic, like much of his collecting activity. However, this did not constitute a collation of the debris from the contemporary London art market, but rather a series of carefully considered investments in the cream of the crop. The result is a drawings collection that is well balanced across a variety of periods, geographies and subject matters. The only exception to this balance within the collection is the vast office drawings collection of Robert and James Adam, which numbers 9,000 sheets and outnumbers even Soane's own office drawings. However, it was with due thought that Soane brought the Adam drawings into his museum, having first declined their purchase and then negotiated an excellent price at which the graphic output of such an influential past architect must have been irresistible.

Together the amassed collection of drawings at the Soane Museum comprises one of the most significant in Britain. Most remain in exquisite condition as for almost two centuries they have lain largely undisturbed. It is only in recent decades – since 1995 with the creation of the museum's first exhibition gallery – that temporary exhibitions have allowed the display of drawings to the public under carefully controlled conditions, albeit in very limited numbers.

Thanks to generous funding from the Leon Levy Foundation, since 2010 the Soane Museum has been able to create a comprehensive archive of digital photography that represents the entire drawings collection. This both facilitates scholarly cataloguing and interpretation of the drawings, allowing us all to better understand the content of this significant national asset, and it has also enabled online publication of the entire drawings collection for public benefit, giving unprecedented, free access to these fragile works without any danger of damage. But even despite all this, the wider public might not feel inclined to peruse an online catalogue without specific cause, and the drawings collection remains a largely hidden and perhaps lesser known facet of the wider collection.

It is my great privilege to work on and with Soane's drawings collection every day and I am keen to share its riches with a wider audience. While it is not possible to illustrate even 1 per cent of Soane's drawings collection in this publication, I hope that it will nonetheless offer the reader a glimpse of the most exceptional among the hidden masterpieces that are to be found within the drawings collection at the Soane Museum.

↓ Joseph Michael Gandy for Sir John Soane, *Various designs for Public and Private buildings 1780–1815*, being an architectural composition of framed perspectives and models of designs by Sir John Soane, exhibited RA 1818, SM P87. Photograph: A.C. Cooper.

Soane office drawings

The drawings from Soane's own architectural practice are almost as varied as the wider collection itself. Not only was he a prolific architect of pre-eminent skill, necessitating the production of seemingly endless designs for his many commissions, but he was also a teacher and prominent member of the RA, elected ARA in 1795 and RA in 1802. Soane exhibited at the RA with impressive regularity, usually with drawings of his architectural designs in the hand of Joseph Michael Gandy.

Gandy worked in Soane's office as a draughtsman between 1798 and 1801, following which he established his own practice, but returned to Soane in a freelance capacity whenever he was needed to produce magnificent drawings. Gandy was elected ARA in 1803 and exhibited his own work, principally history paintings, almost every year between 1800 and 1838, meaning that he often exhibited there in a dual capacity under both Soane's name and his own. Certainly, Soane had good reason to favour Gandy as he had a reputation for excellence. When landscape painter and diarist Joseph Farington visited sculptor Joseph Nollekens on Saturday 5 November 1803, he recounted in his diary a conversation in which Nollekens recalled Joseph Bonomi naming Gandy 'the best draughtsman in England'. It was through Gandy's skill that Soane was able to illustrate his finest architectural compositions to the best effect, either in elegant single or composite views. However much one of Soane's commissions had been limited by budget or building plot size, Gandy's grandiose RA exhibition drawings could display his architectural designs as Soane had wished them to be: the ideal version of his work, devoid of worldly constraint or the pressures of a client's poor taste, and ignoring the very fact of whether or not a design had even come to fruition.

Much of Soane's characteristically pared-down style was well established by the time Gandy arrived in his office, but Brian Lukacher has noted the radiance of Gandy's drawings and the fact that 'it is extremely difficult to judge the degree to which Gandy's visualizing skills had a determining influence on Soane's experimental approach to spatial form and his unique conflation of Greek and Gothic idioms of architecture.' It must not go unnoticed that Soane chose Gandy's graphic representations of his architecture quite specifically as the method by which his genius would be communicated on a public stage. In Gandy, it seems Soane had found his perfect counterpart, particularly as Soane grew older and his eyesight began to fail; and in Soane, Gandy had found a wealthy patron who could be relied upon to provide regular employment. However, this did not prevent occasional disagreements concerning the creative or intellectual ownership of the drawings exhibited.

Many of the drawings produced by Gandy for exhibition at the RA later found a home among the framed works of art at the Soane Museum. Others were commissioned by Soane specifically for this purpose, sometimes illustrating the interiors of the museum itself. Towards the end of Soane's life, as the Soane Museum came to be viewed by his contemporaries as a national gallery, it is unsurprising that he should exhibit the finest draughtsmanship of the age and, moreover, that Gandy's work should celebrate Soane's own architectural output.

Perhaps slightly less glamorous than Gandy's work, the everyday work of Soane's architectural office usually focused on drawings made in preparation for Soane's various architectural commissions, be they country houses, town houses, churches, monuments or public buildings. Some of Soane's most famous commissions include the rebuilding of the Bank of England and its associated provincial branch banks, various works at the Palace of Westminster, Dulwich Picture Gallery, the Royal Hospital at Chelsea, Pitzhanger Manor in Ealing, Tyringham Hall in Buckinghamshire and Moggerhanger in Bedfordshire, along with a great many others. For each project, be it large or small, it would have been necessary for the office to produce reams of drawings of different configurations. The vast majority of these drawings take the form of an architectural plan, elevation, section or perspective view. For those who are unfamiliar with these terms, a plan is a drawing illustrating the footprint, and also often the internal arrangement of a building on a horizontal plane. An elevation shows a building orthogonally – directly head-on – on a vertical plane. A section cuts through a building at right angles, on a vertical plane, either axially or longitudinally. And a perspective view is a mode of pictorial representation, depicting the subject within a naturalistic composition complete with one or more vanishing points. Each of these methods of drawing appeared in England at different times, but all were commonplace by the seventeenth century. However, by Soane's lifetime it was also typical to utilize the bird's-eye view, the flier or flap, which can overlay an alternative concept on top of an original drawing, and also the laid-out wall elevation, sometimes known as the exploded plan – thought to have been invented by William Kent in 1735 – which offers the walls and floor or ceiling of a single room displayed like an unfolded cardboard cut-out. And so, with all of these different forms of drawing, the Soane office was accustomed to producing material of a considerable variety.

Naturally, some of these drawing formats are easier for the layperson to 'read' or interpret than others and, as such, certain drawing types predominated in eighteenth- and nineteenth-century British architectural practices, depending on whether a drawing was intended for use within the office or for the perusal of the client. It is for this reason that perspective or bird's-eye views, complete with a suitable topographical context, were popular for engraving and publication as they are as undemanding and straightforward to the layperson as a picture postcard.

However, the Soane office would not simply produce one copy of each drawing. Indeed, by this date the typical architectural process of design and drawing production was multi-layered. The first task was to send a trusted draughtsman to the building site in order to make survey drawings of any pre-existing architecture, or perhaps simply the topography of the building site, in order to provide the architect – in this case Soane himself – with the relevant information needed in order to undertake his designs. Survey drawings take different forms, but as their principal function is to relay an accurate representation, they are often drawn simply but to scale, or thoroughly dimensioned and without any unnecessary ornamental flourishes that might distract or confuse.

Next the actual process of design would begin. The first phase of the design process was almost exclusively the territory of the architect rather than his draughtsman. Soane himself would produce the earliest preliminary designs as a means of developing his initial ideas, often simply sketched in pencil or pen to a rough scale and without the hindrance of wash. Such sketches would then be passed along to the draughtsmen in order to work up the design, draw it to scale and thereby translate Soane's freehand sketch into a more cohesive design. Such drawings are often overdrawn and annotated by Soane himself as the design evolved.

Once Soane was satisfied with the various elements of any given design it was then necessary to produce a finished or fair drawing, providing a fully worked-up, neat version of the design, drawn to scale, usually washed in grey or colour, and often produced by more than one draughtsman depending on the differing skills of each person. If this version of the design was considered by Soane to be of sufficient quality, it would be presented to the client – be they an individual or a committee – as a means of explaining and promoting the design idea. The hope was that he, she or they would invest in Soane's architectural vision and that the design would be executed. However, there are numerous finished drawings within the Soane office collection, which, for one reason or another, were not deemed by Soane to be appropriate

for the client and, as such, it was common for multiple copies and versions of finished drawings to be produced. Where there is evidence that a drawing had achieved the draughtsman's goal and been found worthy of Soane's clients, then it is known as a presentation drawing, because it was 'presented' to the client.

Presentation drawings were sometimes submitted to architectural competitions in a bid to win a commission. However, it must also be remembered that not all drawing competitions were so mercenary, for example, the annual RA student competition. Soane himself had won the RA gold medal for architecture in 1776, for an exquisite drawing illustrating his design for a monumental bridge.

Should a client be pleased with the drawings and instruct Soane to contract craftsmen in order to execute the design, then it was necessary for an entirely new series of drawings to be produced. Presentation drawings made for the client were considered to be works of art, conveying a concept in the most alluring means possible, but not necessarily providing enough detailed information for the building process. As such, it was then necessary for the office to provide a series of working drawings, which would each deal with one small element of the design. Drawn to scale and annotated with all the relevant information that the builder or craftsman might need, working drawings provided comprehensive design instructions to the executant artisan in order that the design might be faithfully reproduced in three dimensions. In the words of Edwin Lutyens, 'a working drawing is merely a letter to a builder telling him precisely what is required of him – and not a picture wherewith to charm an idiotic client'. After all, it would be no use if the drawings alone were captivatingly elegant, only for the finished building to fall short of the client's expectations.

During the eighteenth century, the administration of most architectural offices had become increasingly meticulous, and it was typical to maintain a series of office record drawings that

would duplicate the designs offered to various clients. This would be done for two obvious reasons: firstly, to document those designs that had actually been sent to a client; and secondly, to prevent any embarrassing repetition in the work provided to different clients. Record drawings were usually made with care, drawn to scale, albeit often reduced in size from a presentation drawing as paper was expensive, and they were often only partially washed or annotated with notations of colour in order to provide all the necessary information while maintaining a maximum of economy. As record drawings represent a design that was perceived to be complete, they are rarely overdrawn with alterations, and were often made and kept in groups or mounted together into volumes. There are 18 surviving volumes of Soane office record drawings in the Soane Museum collection.

Ever since his early days in the architectural profession, Soane had been in the habit of making reduced-scale duplicates of his designs for record-keeping purposes, and former Soane Museum Curator Margaret Richardson has suggested that he had learned to do this in the office of the architect Henry Holland (1745–1806), for whom Soane had served as an assistant and draughtsman in 1772–8, prior to his Grand Tour. There are a great many similarities between the small-scale format of Soane's early record drawings and those from the Holland office, now in the RIBA drawings collection. It was in the mid-1780s that Soane's record drawings became slightly larger – presumably as by this time his office could afford the use of larger, more expensive sheets of paper – and these were mounted in more formal record volumes. In the late 1790s, these record volumes were divided by town and country projects, doubtless as Soane was anxious to publish his work and needed to assemble his designs in an appropriate arrangement.

The publication of architectural designs had been commonplace since the early eighteenth century and particularly since Colen Campbell's publication of *Vitruvius Britannicus* in 1715–25. Like many of his predecessors, Soane was keen on architectural treatises as a means of disseminating and advertising his work. He produced seven publications during the course of his career, including *Plans of Buildings Erected in the Counties of Norfolk, Suffolk, etc.* in 1788; *Designs for Public and Private Buildings* in 1828; *Plans, Elevations and Perspective Views of Pitzhanger Manor House* in 1833; *Memoirs of the Professional Life of an Architect* in 1835; and *Descriptions of the House and Museum at Lincoln's Inn Fields* in 1830, 1832 and 1835. Graphic material for illustrating publications was produced in the form of engravings, with Soane providing his engraver with a series of drawings from which to work. Clearly, the drawings made for publication – similar to those produced for exhibition – illustrated only those designs with which the author was most pleased, whether they had been executed or not. They tended to be produced as orthogonal or topographical elevations, simple plans and perspective or bird's-eye views, but rarer are more complex plans and sections, which are detailed with structural complexities and are therefore more difficult for the layperson to comprehend.

In order to keep pace with the vast number of drawings needed to fulfil Soane's various commissions and indeed publications, the office grew quite considerably as time progressed. From September 1784, Soane began to accept articled pupils whom he instructed in the Art, Profession and Business of architecture. He took his pedagogical responsibilities extremely seriously; stressing the importance of superior draughtsmanship techniques, accurate and honest estimates of costs and a profound understanding of construction and building materials. The pupils' day generally comprised running errands and undertaking drawing work – architectural training drawings comprising yet another interesting type of graphic representation – but from 1810 onwards the pupils would also be fortunate enough to visit Soane's building sites, having been tasked with the production of so-called progress drawings. A rough sketch was made *in situ* and then on returning to the office this would be redrawn more formally and washed in colour. Seemingly rare at the time, progress drawings were a means of recording the evolving construction process on a building site. With only a handful of precedents in Britain, it is likely that this form of drawing had been inspired by the works of Piranesi – particularly his *Carceri d'Invenzione* (1749) and *Le Antichità Romane* (1756) – as well as European medieval and Renaissance manuscripts containing illustrations of craftsmen at work. Soane himself owned a sixteenth-century illuminated Flemish *Book of Hours* that illustrates the construction of the Tower of Babel (see page 26).

We might assume that the rationale for the production of progress drawings was for Soane himself to be updated on progress, although this would more typically fall within the remit of a project's Clerk of Works. Soane's pupils only made progress drawings on building sites within Greater London (the Bank of England, Dulwich Picture Gallery, the Royal Hospital at Chelsea and the Soane family tomb) all within walking distance of Soane's office in Lincoln's Inn Fields. They did not go further afield for this purpose, for example, to Soane's country house projects. Clearly the production of progress drawings was not a comprehensive undertaking across the office's works. It is likely that Soane's intentions were didactic and driven by a desire for his pupils to scrutinize building sites, construction processes and the application of varied building materials. This was part of their training. Indeed, in Soane's own words:

> *By attending the progress of buildings and by making drawings of them in their different stages of progress the Student will not only attain great skill in the mechanism of building, but at the same time discover many effects of light and shade, which a closer observation of nature alone can give.*
> (Sir John Soane, RA lecture 12.)

In 1806, at the age of 53 and acclaimed for his architectural achievements, Soane was elected Professor of Architecture at the Royal Academy. This was an ideal calling for an architect who treated the education of his own office apprentices with such care. He compiled a series of 12 lectures for the RA, to be delivered at a rate of 6 per year, detailing the history of architecture and offering his opinions on the best and worst examples of the craft. As the Napoleonic Wars raged across the English Channel, it would have been unwise, if not impossible, for Soane's RA students to attempt Continental travel in order to peruse the architectural delights of Italy and beyond, as Soane had done himself. So, in order to address this failing in their education, Soane instructed his own office to create almost 1,000 large-scale lecture drawings, illustrating significant buildings from across the reaches of history and geography. These would not only illustrate Soane's words, but also function as case studies of the key principles of the architectural profession. A suitable selection of these drawings would be displayed in the Great Exhibition Room at Somerset House during each of Soane's RA lectures. And from 1812 Soane invited his students to peruse both the lecture drawings and his wider collection at Lincoln's Inn Fields on the days before and after each of his lectures.

Soane had been inspired to create his RA lecture drawings by the example of Thomas Sandby (1721–98), Professor of Architecture at the RA when he was a student. But whereas Sandby produced some 128 lecture drawings, Soane's efforts were on an entirely different scale. Without any remuneration from the RA, this extraordinary collection was produced on a purely philanthropic basis and is thought to comprise the earliest attempt at a graphic history of world architecture. The drawings provided the RA students with the ultimate teaching aid: a Grand Tour in microcosm. As we know, Soane was an ardent advocate of architectural education, the lecture drawings being yet more evidence of this conviction, but they also offer a glimpse of his personality and most cherished values. Having been produced principally by his office apprentices through observation of drawings and engravings in his collection, Soane was providing employment to his office, particularly for the younger, aspiring members of that group, during the otherwise relatively lean years of the Napoleonic Wars. Instead of reducing the number of people in his employ, Soane engineered work for them to do, which he funded himself, and that resulted in one of the most masterful pedagogical efforts of his generation.

Office of Sir John Soane, RA lecture drawing, the caryatids on the Erechtheum, Athens, 1806–19, SM 24/4/1. Photograph: Ardon Bar-Hama.

Drawings collecting and provenance

Prior to his professorship at the RA, Soane had been relatively cautious in collecting drawings, and it was indeed his teaching activities that spurred him to collect more enthusiastically, presumably so as to provide additional educational material. Having said this, Soane probably first encountered a collection of drawings during his apprenticeship with the skilled and progressive architect George Dance the Younger. The very fact that Soane later kept Dance's office drawings in a piece of furniture called the 'shrine' suggests his reverence both for Dance and this medium of art. Soane was a true connoisseur, and from 1810 onwards he acquired all manner of drawings by, among many others, Alberto Alberti (1525–98), Giovanni Battista Montano (1534–1621), John Thorpe (c.1565–1655), Johannes Lutma (c.1584–1669), Henry Stone (1616–53), Carlo Fontana (c.1634–1714), Nicholas Hawksmoor, Grinling Gibbons (1648–1721), Leonard Knyff (1650–1722), William Talman (1650–1719), Sir James Thornhill (c.1675–1734), James Gibbs (1682–1754) and William Kent (1685–1748), as well as his closer contemporaries John Michael Rysbrack (1694–1770), Agostino Carlini (c.1718–90), Giovanni Battista Piranesi, Thomas Sandby, Charles-Louis Clérisseau (1721–1820), Sir William Chambers, Sir Joshua Reynolds (1723–92), Antonio Zucchi (1726–95), Robert Adam (1728–92), Giuseppe Manocchi (1731–82), Joseph Nollekens (1737–1823), John Linnell (1739–1810), Joseph Bonomi the Elder (1739–1808), George Dance, Charles Cameron (1745–1812), Humphry Repton (1752–1818) and James Playfair (1755–94). These names span an array of professions including those of architect, draughtsman, painter, sculptor, cabinetmaker and garden designer. Added to these drawings was a variety of volumes including the famous *Codex Coner* and a series of illuminated manuscripts, including one illustrated by the pre-eminent Croatian master, Giulio Clovio (1498–1578).

By the time of his death in January 1837, Soane's drawings collection was composed of around 30,000 sheets, resulting in the first comprehensive architectural drawings collection in Britain, preserving the finest examples of drawings from the Renaissance through to Georgian Britain. It is with complete confidence that the Soane Museum can claim one of the two foremost collections of architectural drawings in Britain, alongside that of the RIBA collection, which was directly inspired by the Soane Museum. It is quite remarkable to think that this was the compilation of a single tireless man.

The origin and provenance of some of Soane's drawings is lost to the mists of time, but for many there are interesting and detailed stories to be told. The provenance of many of the drawings included in this volume are set out in the image captions, but in this introduction it seems appropriate to give details of the history of a selection of the most significant drawings in Soane's collection.

John Thorpe volume

Soane's first, cautious foray into collecting drawings in Britain took place on 10 January 1795 when he acquired 286 drawings by the architect James Playfair at Christie's. These include designs for Kinnaird Castle in Angus and Dalkeith House in Midlothian. This was followed two years later by the purchase of 20 *capricci* by the French artist Charles-Louis Clérisseau. But later, following the watershed of Soane's election as Professor of Architecture at the RA in 1806, the acquisition of drawings gained increased momentum. The first purchase to mark this shift was that of a volume of drawings by the Elizabethan architect John Thorpe, who was a member of the Office of Works as well as being responsible for a number of houses including the original Holland House in Kensington and parts of Audley End in Essex.

Much admired in the eighteenth century by the politician, writer and antiquarian Horace Walpole, the Thorpe volume is widely thought to be the most important collection of drawings to survive from the Elizabethan or Jacobean era, rivalled only by the Smythson Collection at the RIBA. The early provenance of the volume is unknown, but the former Soane Museum Curator Sir John Summerson suggested that it passed during Thorpe's lifetime to Fulke Greville (later Baron Brooke of Beauchamp Court), who was granted Warwick Castle by King James I in 1604 and was a great student of the arts. If this were the case, the volume might have lain undisturbed at Warwick Castle until the mid-eighteenth century and the time of the 8th Baron Brooke (later 1st Earl of Warwick) who undertook architectural improvements there. It was at this time that Walpole visited Warwick Castle and discovered the Thorpe volume, announcing his triumph to the world in 1782 in a supplement to the 3rd edition of his *Anecdotes of Paintings in England*:

> *By the favour of the Earl of Warwick, I am enabled to bring to light a very capital artist, who designed or improved most of the principal and palatial edifices erected in the reigns of Elizabeth and James I, though even his name was totally forgotten, I am empowered by the same condescension to point out a volume of drawings of that individual architect John Thorpe, who has left a folio of plans, now in Lord Warwick's possession.*

Following an enquiry from the antiquarian John Britton (1771–1857) in 1809, the 2nd Earl of Warwick was unable to find the Thorpe volume at Warwick Castle. This was explained the following year when it appeared at Christie's, in the sale of possessions belonging to the late Charles Francis Greville, the Earl's younger brother. Soane purchased the volume at that sale for 27½ guineas, but immediately wrote to the Earl offering its return to Warwick Castle, only to receive a courteous response requesting that Soane keep it. Although Soane mentioned the Thorpe volume in his fifth RA lecture, he was not keen for scholars to consult the drawings, considering the Elizabeth style to represent a poor form of architecture and a debased version of classicism. Soane's draughtsman, Charles James Richardson (1806–71), had much more interest in Thorpe and gained permission from the Soane Museum Trustees, following Soane's death, to make tracings in preparation for publication. However, this never came to fruition and it was not until 1966, with Sir John Summerson's publication of the entire volume, that it was made available to the public.

Sir William Chambers

The next significant purchase of drawings took place only one year later at a sale of the possessions of the eighteenth-century architect Sir William Chambers. There are now over 800 drawings by Chambers within the collection at the Soane Museum, but it is quite clear that not all of these came to Soane from the 1811 sale, where he spent only £14.11.0. His purchases did include two exceptional examples: Chambers's design for a mausoleum for Frederick, Prince of Wales made in 1751, and a drawing of Nicola Salvi's (1697–1751) Trevi Fountain in Rome, which had been a collaborative effort in 1753 between Chambers and the French artist Laurent Pécheux (1729–1821).

There are over 600 Chambers drawings for Somerset House now in the collection at the Soane Museum and these were bought in the 1811 sale for £52.10.0, but not by Soane. Rather, the Somerset House drawings were sold to an unknown person named Townley. There is no evidence as to how the Somerset House drawings came into the Soane Museum's collection before Soane's death 26 years later, although a handful of other Chambers drawings were acquired by Soane in a piecemeal fashion between 1816 and 1827 from John Britton. It has been pointed out by Sue Palmer, the Soane Museum Archivist, that Soane's acquisition of the Somerset House drawings may have taken place quite late in his life. The first Soane Museum Curator, George Bailey (1792–1860), compiled a *Classified Catalogue of the Library* in the years immediately following Soane's death in which he referred to the 'original Drawings of Somerset House [...] not yet bound up', suggesting that Soane had never had the chance to arrange the drawings in his customary fashion.

Robert and James Adam

The next significant acquisitions of drawings in Soane's collecting career took place in 1818 and included some of the most important items now at the Soane Museum. These all came via the collection of the Scottish architect Robert Adam. Now remembered as one of the innovators of Neo-classicism in Britain, Adam was the most prolific architect of the eighteenth century, but his finances were extremely strained in the last 20 years of his life because of the failure of a major speculative town-planning development in London, known as the Adelphi. At his death in 1792, the Neo-classical Adam style had still been popular, but within ten years fashion had changed to such an extent that there was little interest in anything the Adam office had to offer. When Robert's partner-brother, James, died in 1794, their property and possessions were inherited by the youngest Adam brother, William, and two spinster sisters, Elizabeth and Margaret, who had acted as Robert and James's housekeepers. Despite the arrival of their niece Susannah Clerk in 1810, who came to care for the three elderly siblings, the family's financial situation was precarious. William had been declared bankrupt in 1801 owing to the remaining debts from the Adelphi. In order to keep themselves afloat, William arranged for the sale at Christie's of Robert and James's library and art collection in 1818, and their personal effects in 1821.

Soane purchased heavily at the 1818 Adam sale, including numerous books and drawings, and perhaps the most significant among these were items from the seventeenth-century Cassiano dal Pozzo Paper Museum. Cassiano dal Pozzo (1588–1657) is now celebrated as one of the greatest patrons of the arts ever to have lived.

Born in Turin but residing principally in Rome, Dal Pozzo had close ties to the Medici. He collected widely, but it was his museum of works on paper that attracted most attention and following his death it passed through his family until it was sold in 1703 for 4,000 *scudi* to Pope Clement XI, and then in 1714 to the Albani family for the same sum. The Albani were already in possession of a significant collection to which they allowed eighteenth-century scholars access for their personal study. During his Grand Tour of 1754–58, Robert Adam had visited the Albani collection and opened negotiations for its purchase on behalf of King George III; this being concluded by his brother James Adam (1732–94) in 1762 for 14,000 *scudi*. On 10 July 1762 James wrote to Robert confirming the purchase not only on behalf of the King, but also of a selection of items for the brothers' personal use, later purchased by Soane at the 1818 Adam sale. These items comprise three volumes of drawings by Giovanni Battista Montano, the *Codex Coner* containing drawings by Bernardo della Volpaia, a volume of drawings by Alberti and the so-called *Vasari Album* containing drawings by Teofilo Torri (1554–1623) and Orazio Porta (*b*.1540). At the same time in 1818, Soane had also purchased loose drawings by Jean-Baptiste Lallemand (1716–1803), Charles-Louis Clérisseau, Laurent Pécheux, Giovanni Battista Piranesi, Robert Adam himself, Paul Sandby (1731–1809) and William Kent, as well as a volume of drawings by Carlo Fontana, all of which had been in the Adam brothers' collection.

Elizabeth Adam died in 1796, followed by Margaret in 1820 and finally William in 1822, leaving their niece, Susannah Clerk, to inherit the one surviving treasure that had remained in the family's possession: the Adam office drawings collection. These drawings were of a consistently high quality as the Adam office employed only professional draughtsmen and never took on students. The sculptor John Flaxman (1755–1826) had advised the family that the Adam office drawings collection was worth 500 guineas, and William had made repeated efforts to sell the drawings in the 1820s, even editing and rearranging the drawings into typologically-arranged folios in the hope of making them more saleable. However, with the Adam style out of fashion and the drawings not yet old enough to attract any antiquarian interest, they remained unsold and were inherited by Susannah. She first offered them to the British Museum, who declined, and then took them with her to Edinburgh where she went to live with her bachelor brother, the Scottish judge Lord Eldin, at 16 Picardy Place. Further attempts were made to sell the Adam drawings at the extraordinarily popular sale of Eldin's possessions in 1833, but to no avail, and finally in that year Susannah approached Soane who had just applied for the Act of Parliament under which he left his museum to the nation. After much indecision, Soane purchased the entire surviving Adam office drawings collection, comprising 54 volumes, for £200. A further three volumes of Adam drawings in the Soane collection are composed of the loose sheets purchased in 1818, and a handful purchased at the Nash sale in 1835, totalling 57 volumes containing 9,000 drawings: over 80 per cent of the surviving Adam drawings in the world.

George Dance the Elder and George Dance the Younger

The final phase of Soane's drawings collecting took place following his decision to leave the museum to the nation in 1833, 'for settling and preserving the Museum for the Benefit of the Public' with provision for 'Amateurs and students … for consulting and inspecting and benefiting by the said collection'. To this day, not only is the Soane Museum open to the public, but the Research Library also offers privileged access to the archives, books and drawings collections by appointment, and the digitally-illustrated online catalogues provide worldwide free access to everyone.

From 1833 onwards, Soane had few outstanding architectural responsibilities and instead he focused on increasing the range and volume of his drawings collection. With the assistance of the antiquarian John Britton, Soane negotiated purchases from a variety of sources. Moreover, with the Soane Museum's growing reputation as a national institution, many people made Soane a gift of drawings, or wrote to him to offer drawings for sale. These included C.H. Tatham who sent drawings by Sir Christopher Wren (1632–1723) and Nicholas Hawksmoor for Greenwich Royal Hospital in 1833; receiving £10 in return.

The last major drawings collection to arrive at the Soane Museum rather neatly closed the circle of Soane's professional life. On 18 November 1836, just weeks before he died on 20 January 1837, Soane paid the generous sum of £500 for the drawings collection of his former master George Dance the Younger. This comprised 1,342 drawings from Dance's own office, 277 prints and six volumes of drawings in other hands, including drawings

by George Dance the Elder (c.1694–1768). On 31 March 1836, George Dance the Younger's son, Lieutenant-Colonel Sir Charles Webb Dance, had written to Soane in order to offer him the collection:

> *I have examined all my dear Father's Drawings which are very voluminous & in high preservation – the Architectural Library is also a very excellent one. Were I not very much reduced in my finances I wd have felt inclined to follow your noble example by presenting this (I think I may say) very valuable collection to be deposited in your National Gallery but having four sons to educate & bring up (besides three daughters) … I shd be neither doing my duty to myself or to them, if I were to part with this, my dear Father's collection without a very handsome consideration.*
> (SM Archives Private Correspondence III.D.5.31)

Clearly Soane felt some obligation of generosity to the son of his old friend. Happily, the Dance collection was housed within a fine piece of furniture, designed by Dance himself, and known as the shrine. At the time of Soane's death this was located in the Library-Dining Room of the museum, but it was moved three times, and since around 1969–71 it has been in the North Drawing Room. Placed in the centre of the room, this large piece of furniture is a forcible and welcome reminder to all of the museum's visitors of the importance that Soane placed on his collection of drawings.

DRAWINGS FROM THE COLLECTION OF SIR JOHN SOANE

The Soane Museum is in possession of the first comprehensive drawings collection compiled in Britain. Unsurprisingly, considering Soane's profession, it is largely architectural in subject matter. However, the collection is impressively diverse, representing the early Renaissance through to Soane's own lifetime and with examples from countries as widespread as Italy and India.

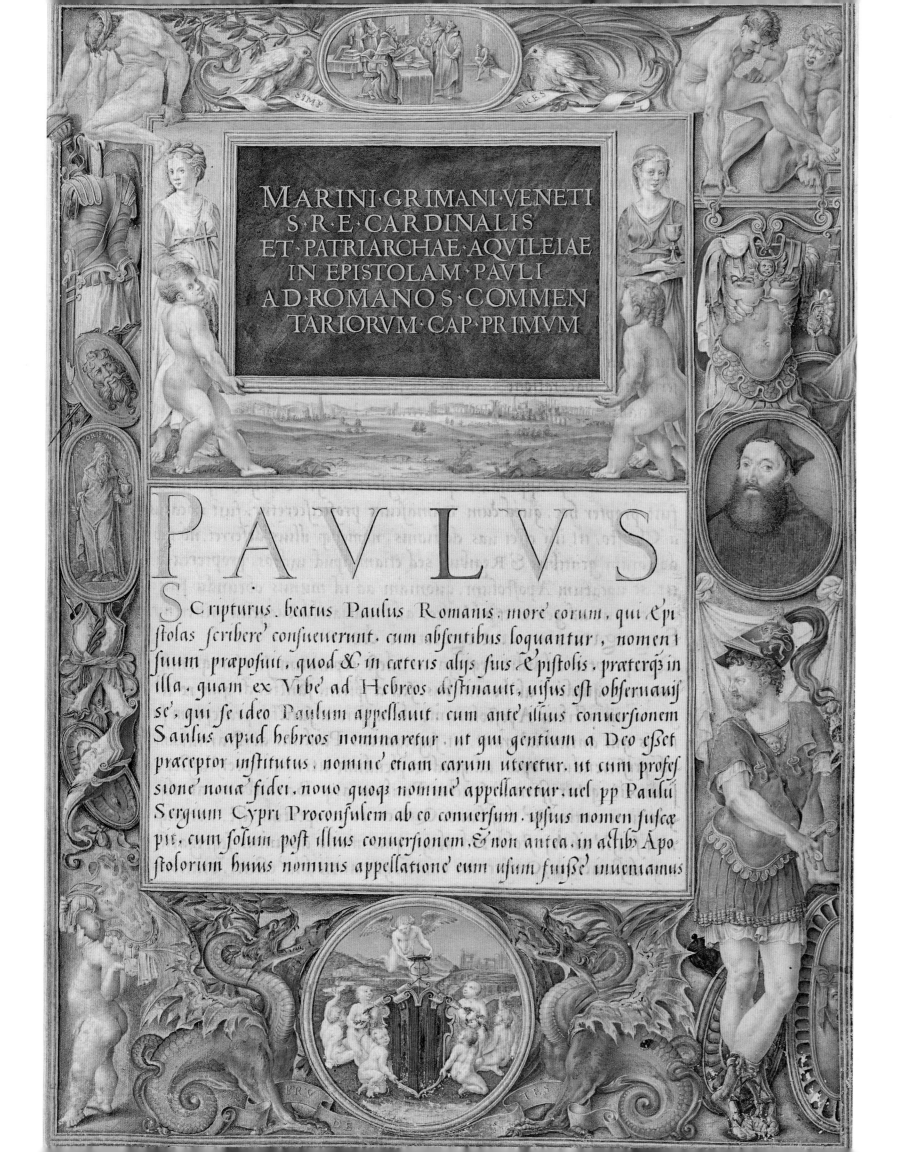

●— Giulio Clovio, illuminations in Cardinal Marino Grimani's *Commentary on the Epistle of St Paul to the Romans*, c.1537–8, SM volume 143/7 verso-8 recto. Photographs: Ardon Bar-Hama.

Giulio Clovio was a Croatian painter and illuminator active in Italy during the sixteenth century. Later in the sixteenth century, Giorgio Vasari described him as the finest miniaturist of all time and certainly today Clovio is widely considered a national Croatian hero – his importance for Croatians is akin to that of Shakespeare to the British. This manuscript was made for Cardinal Grimani in whose household Clovio had trained as a painter from an early age under Giulio Romano. The volume contains miniatures by Clovio and astonishingly beautiful calligraphy by his assistant, Francesco Monteschi, all applied to vellum. The borders of these two plates were inspired by Raphael's lost tapestry cartoons of the Conversion of Saul, which had been in the collection of Cardinal Grimani's uncle. Of particular interest on the first page, in the centre of the left-hand side, we can see a roundel depicting St Paul holding a sword and a book, and on the second page, in the centre of the right-hand border, we can see a portrait of Cardinal Grimani himself. The principal framed image depicts the conversion of St Paul. The volume was purchased from the Grimani family library in the eighteenth century by Consul Joseph Smith, who was doubtless responsible for bringing it to England. It then passed through several hands and was sold to Soane in 1833 by the Duke of Buckingham.

●— **Flemish School: two artists, illumination showing the construction of the Tower of Babel from a Book of Hours, after 1512, SM volume 137/26 recto. Photograph: Geremy Butler.**
Books of Hours were used by Roman Catholics, particularly wealthy women, from the medieval period onwards, as a means of instructing personal prayer at particular canonical times of the day. The wealthier the owner or donor of the Book of Hours, the more opulently they were illuminated. There is a note in German and Latin within this early sixteenth-century Flemish example, which explains that it was made as a gift for Johanna, wife of Fernando of Aragon, from Wolfgang Wilhelm, Count Palatine of Neuberg, and therefore it is of the highest quality. Containing illuminations by two different artists, but carefully arranged in order that the plates should be relevant to the adjacent text, this volume was clearly created as a single entity rather than cannibalized from other sources. Each illumination follows the same three-quarter page format, with the subjects for these images lifted from both the Old and New Testaments. Each is paired with another suitable illumination. This plate illustrates the construction of the Tower of Babel and is paired with an image of Pentecost. Annotations within the volume show that it later belonged to Edward Knight, at the sale of whose possessions on 10 May 1821 it was purchased by Richard, 1st Duke of Buckingham (fourth creation). It was finally sold to Soane in September 1833 by the Duke, Soane's client at Stowe, for the colossal sum of £735, along with a late fifteenth-century *Book of Hours of the Blessed Virgin Mary*, written for use in Tours, France, and Marino Grimani's sixteenth-century *Commentary on the Epistle of St Paul to the Romans*.

—• **Attributed to the Master of Mantegna, elevations of a pilaster and two entablatures, sixteenth century, SM volume 114/11. Photograph: Ardon Bar-Hama.**

Attributed to the so-called Master of Mantegna, whose work can be found in a sketchbook in the Kunstbibliothek in Berlin, this drawing of ornamental details depicts a foliate pilaster incorporating dolphins and two elaborate entablatures, all of which are probably derived from unknown antique sources. Although not visible here, the right-hand corners of the sheet are rounded, suggesting that it was once a leaf within a sketchbook, perhaps a pattern book of antique decorative motifs. It was certainly made within a studio environment rather than from observation *in situ* as the paper has been carefully incised prior to the application of ink. The drawing is contained within the *Margaret Chinnery Album*, which is a scrapbook album of Italian and Northern European Renaissance drawings of architecture and interior decorative motifs by a variety of artists, seemingly assembled in the seventeenth century. It is named after an inscription on the first folio in an eighteenth-century hand. Margaret Chinnery was the wife of one of Soane's clients, William Bassett Chinnery of Gillwell Hall in Essex, for whom he had made improvements to a London townhouse on Mortimer Street. Chinnery was a noted patron of the arts, but in 1812 was found to have embezzled £81,000 from the Treasury and fled to the Continent. Soane attended a sale of the couple's possessions on 7 June 1812, but this volume was not included. Lynda Fairbairn has suggested that Soane acquired the volume earlier than the 1812 sale in lieu of architect's fees for his work at Mortimer Street.

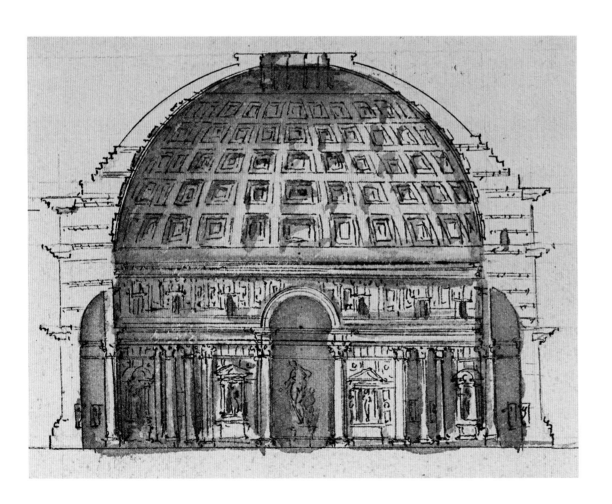

●━● **Giovanni Battista Montano after Andrea Palladio, plan, elevation, section and details of the Pantheon, Rome, *c.*1540– 1621, SM volume 124/61. Photograph: Ardon Bar-Hama.**

Giovanni Battista Montano produced this drawing of the Pantheon after a plate from Andrea Palladio's *I quattro libri dell'architecttura … (1570)*. Montano worked principally as a woodcarver, but also had considerable skill as a draughtsman, architect and model-maker. Although he was a member of the Accademia di San Luca where he exercised considerable influence through his lectures on architecture, and worked for a number of prominent clients, including Fernando de' Medici, Grand Duke of Tuscany in 1598– 1601, none of Montano's woodcarving or architectural work survives and he never found fame during the course of his life. It was the quality of his drawings – many illustrating antique buildings – for which he received posthumous notoriety. Although we do not know why Montano made these drawings in the first place, they were edited by a former architectural collaborator, Giovanni Battista Soria, who published a selection of them from 1624 in *Li cinque libri di architettura di Gio. Battista Montani Milanese …* At some time before his death, Soria sold Montano's drawings to Cassiano dal Pozzo for his paper museum. Three volumes of drawings by Montano from the Dal Pozzo collection were among items purchased by Soane in 1818 at the Adam sale (see page 20).

Cane 6

61

●— Attributed to Hieronymus Cock after the circle of Domenico Ghirlandaio, view of the Colosseum, Rome, *c*.1550, SM volume 114/30. Photograph: Geremy Butler.

The high quality of this drawing, which depicts the exterior of the Colosseum, with glimpses through the arcaded walls into the arena, suggests that it was carefully made for engraving. It has been attributed to the Flemish etcher and publisher, Hieronymus Cock (1518–70), who from 1550 made a series of Roman views for publication from observation of drawings by other artists. In this case the image is certainly taken from the fifteenth-century *Codex Escurialensis*, attributed to the circle of Ghirlandaio and now in the library at San Lorenzo de El Escorial in Madrid. This drawing is contained within the *Margaret Chinnery Album*, which was probably given or sold to Soane in lieu of architect's fees by William Bassett Chinnery (see page 27).

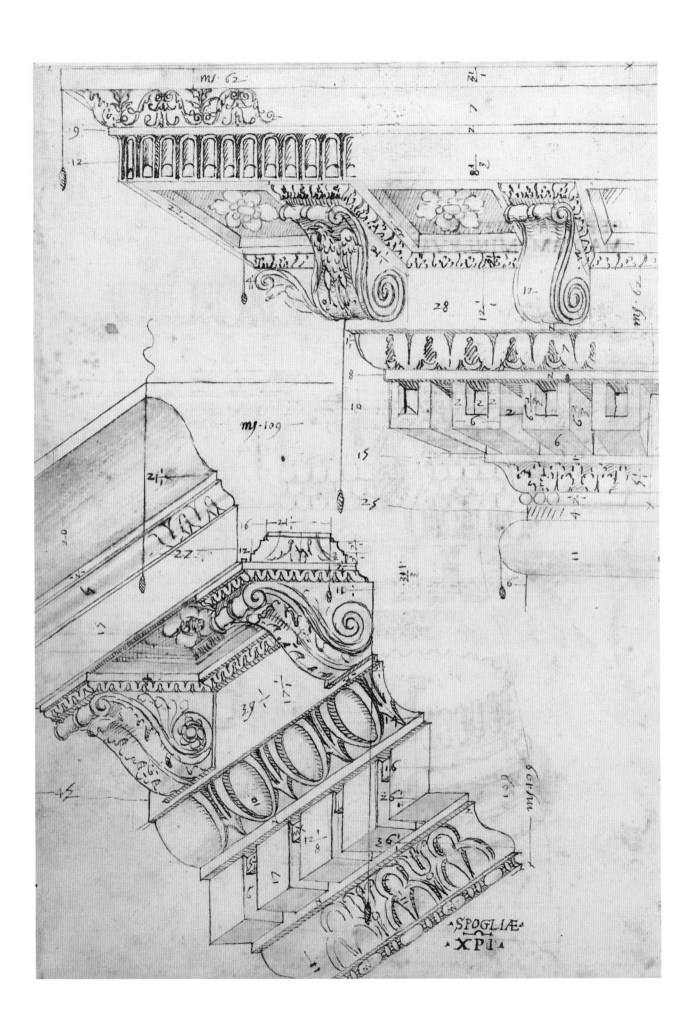

●— Bernardo della Volpaia, elevation and view of entablatures, later sixteenth and seventeenth century, from the *Codex Coner*, SM volume 115/88. Photograph: Ardon Bar-Hama.

The *Codex Coner* is a sixteenth- and seventeenth-century volume of architectural and decorative drawings formerly attributed to a German priest, Andreas Coner, and now considered to be by a Florentine architect, Bernardo della Volpaia (1475–1521) and another later hand. It was borrowed from Volpaia in 1516 by Michelangelo, in an effort to better school himself in architectural detail. There are six drawings by Michelangelo after the *Codex Coner* at the British Museum, London and the Casa Buonaroti, Florence. This Volpaia drawing is one from which Michelangelo made a drawing that survives in the British Museum. It shows the cornices from the Arch of Constantine and the Basilica Ulpia in Rome. The volume was among items purchased by Soane in 1818 at the Adam sale (see page 20).

—• **Giovanni Battista Gisleni, frontispiece for a volume containing designs for buildings in Poland, _c._1649, SM volume 121/1. Photograph: Hugh Kelly.**

Giovanni Battista Gisleni (1600–72) was an Italian architect, stage designer and musician who was attracted to working in Poland in the seventeenth century by the large number of potential clients among the wealthy royal family and aristocracy. Indeed, his epitaph in Santa Maria del Popolo in Rome informs us that he worked for three Polish kings: Sigismund III, Ladislaus IV and John II Casimir. This drawing is the frontispiece to a volume of fine record drawings in Gisleni's hand, giving examples of his designs for domestic and ecclesiastical architecture, interior design and garden furnishings. It was produced as a record of his work for posterity. Presumably Gisleni – like Soane – had some concern for his legacy. Moreover, the volume provides a rare and valuable record of Baroque architecture in Poland, with the frontispiece alone offering a magnificent display of this work, which is scaled by staffage, and includes a banner explaining the contents. There is a pencil inscription on the front free endpaper of the volume, which reads: _116 drawings / £3.3.0_ but further to this, nothing is known of when or how it came into Soane's collection.

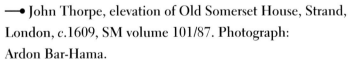
John Thorpe, elevation of Old Somerset House, Strand, London, *c.*1609, SM volume 101/87. Photograph: Ardon Bar-Hama.

John Thorpe (*c.*1565–*c.*1655) was a clerk and surveyor in the Office of Works until 1601 when he established himself in independent practice as an architect. This drawing is contained in a volume comprising a selection of presentation drawings of Thorpe's own work as well as survey drawings of pre-existing, significant buildings, presumably intended for use in discussion with clients. The volume was purchased by Soane in 1810 at the sale of possessions belonging to Charles Francis Greville (see page 19). This drawing depicts proposed alterations to the Strand façade of Old Somerset House, the home of Lord Protector Somerset from 1547–52, which underwent major alterations in 1609–13 for Queen Anne of Denmark. A variant of this design was carried out from 1609, albeit with an additional storey and some ornamental alterations. Old Somerset House was demolished in 1775 in favour of a new scheme by Sir William Chambers.

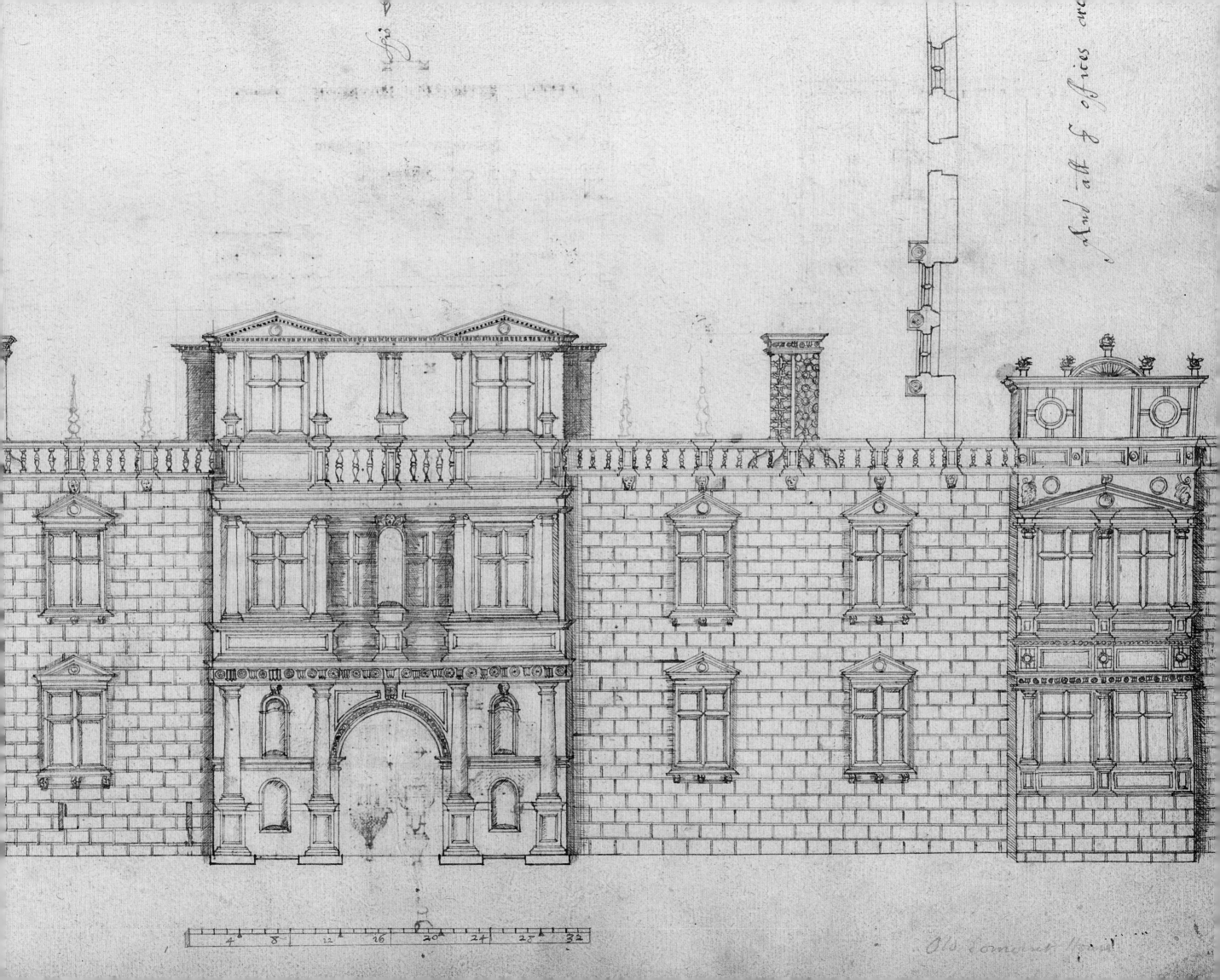

And all of offices are

Old Somerset House

●── Henry Stone, view showing a landscape and figure study made in Italy, 1638–42, SM volume 92/21. Photograph: Ardon Bar-Hama.

Henry Stone was an English painter who visited Italy in 1638–42 with his sculptor brother Nicholas Stone the Younger (*c*.1587–1647), serving as guides to the wealthy collector Sir William Paston of Oxnead Hall, Norfolk. This is a figure study sketch from one of Stone's sketchbooks from that time, which contains 22 leaves of drawings. It appears that this study was made *en plein air*, and presumably depicts the group observing Roman ruins. The sketchbook probably passed to Henry's younger brother John, the last surviving member of the Stone family. Annotations inside the front cover show that it was later acquired by the antiquarian George Vertue, then by the sculptor and architect James Paine junior. Following his death, Paine's collection was sold at Christie's on 12 March 1830, where this, another Stone family sketchbook and two notebooks were purchased for £7.5.0 by a Mr Tiffen – possibly the printseller W.B. Tiffin – who after four days made a considerable profit by selling all four volumes to Soane for £34.15.0.

──● Sir Joshua Reynolds, figurative composition depicting *St Michael overwhelming the demon* within a sketchbook made in Italy, 1751, SM volume 32/183. Photograph: Ardon Bar-Hama.

In the spring of 1749, the portrait painter Sir Joshua Reynolds became acquainted with the Hon. Commodore Augustus Keppel, who offered him passage on the HMS *Centurion* to Italy. There he spent two years studying Old Master paintings, being particularly enamoured of Guido Reni's *Saint Michael the Archangel defeating Satan* (*c*.1632) at Santa Maria della Concezione in Rome. This sketchbook contains a selection of Reynolds's drawings made after artworks he had seen in Italy, with the majority having been made in 1751 during a visit to Bologna on his way back to England. Reynolds inscribed this drawing with the words: *St Michael in St Petronio*, indicating that this depicts Denis Calvaert's *St Michael overwhelming the demon* (1582) in the San Petronio Basilica in Bologna. It is unsurprising that Reynolds should have taken an interest in Calvaert's *St Michael* in Bologna as it is thought to have been the source for Guido Reni's version in Rome 50 years later. Following his return to London, Reynolds's career began to take flight and by the mid-1750s his business as a portrait painter had found enormous success. This meant that by 1768 he had the *gravitas* necessary to play a central role in the foundation of the RA and served as its first President. Soane purchased this extraordinary little sketchbook for £26.5.0 in May 1821, at a sale of the possessions of the Countess of Thomond, Reynolds's niece. Being non-architectural, the Reynolds sketchbook is among the minority of Soane's drawings, but was doubtless of interest to Soane on account of Reynolds's connection with the RA.

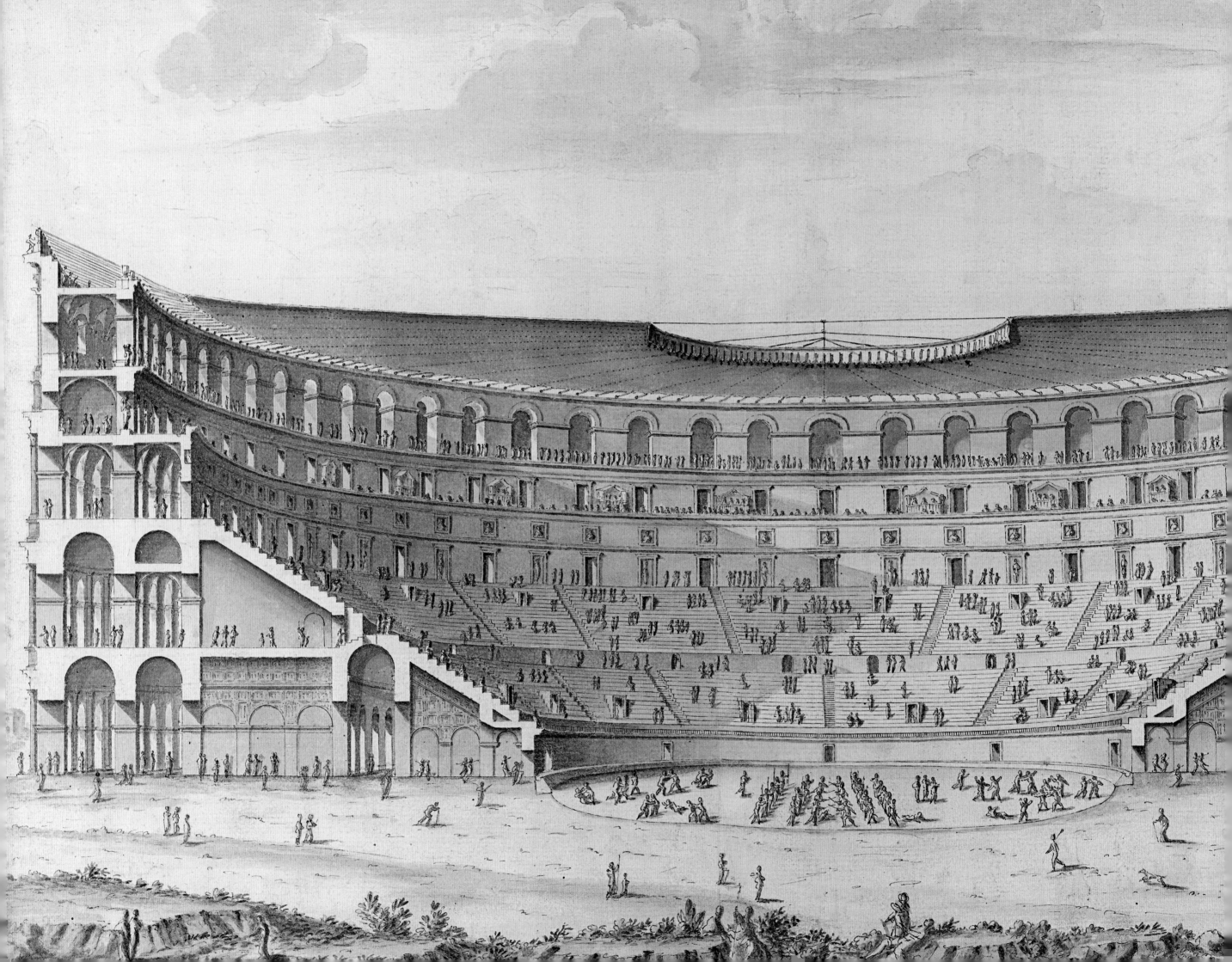

●— Carlo Fontana, section showing a contest in the Colosseum, Rome, *c*.1676–1707, SM volume 116/24. Photograph: Ardon Bar-Hama.

This drawing is one of a set of 26 depicting the Colosseum. It was drawn by the Italian architect, Carlo Fontana, who had it engraved for inclusion in his published monograph on the Colosseum entitled *L'anfiteatro Flavio descritto e delineato dal cavaliere Carlo Fontana*. The engravings were completed by D. Franceschini in 1696, but the publication did not appear until 1725. Soane purchased three copies of the book in 1800, 1801 and 1816, but it was not until 13 July 1830 that he acquired this volume containing Fontana's original drawings, purchased from the antiquarian John Britton for £3.3.0.

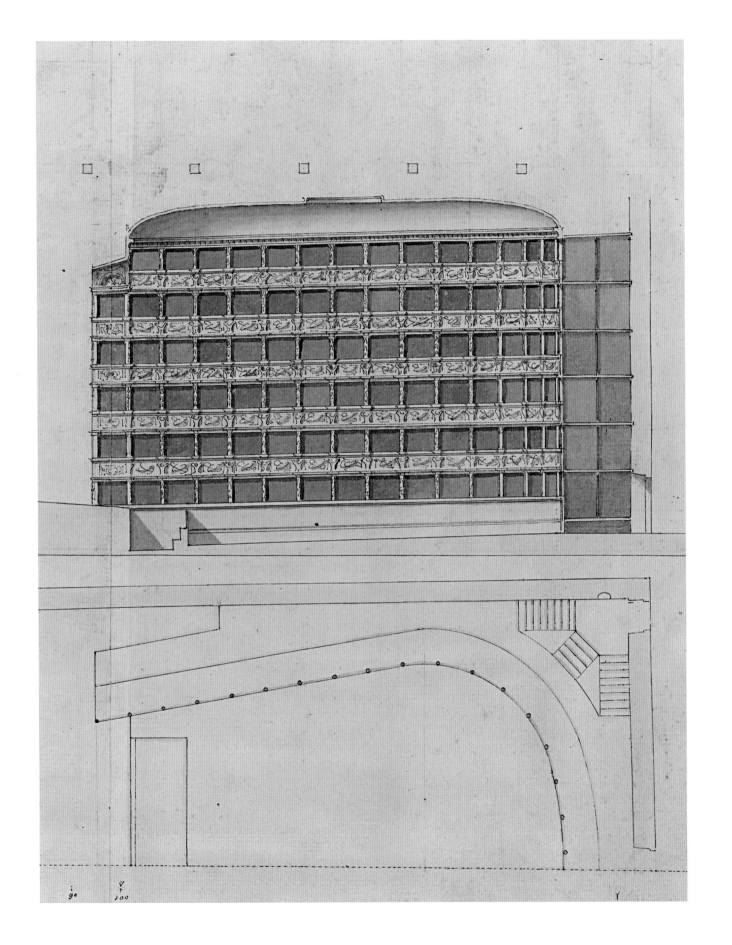

●— Carlo Fontana, plan and section of the Teatro Tor di Nona, Rome, seventeenth century, SM volume 117/6. Photograph: Ardon Bar-Hama.

➡• Tomaso Belli, plan and section of the Theatre of SS. Giovanni e Paolo, Venice, c.1678–96, SM volume 117/34. Photograph: Ardon Bar-Hama.

This drawing depicts a rather technical plan and section of the interior of the Theatre of SS. Giovanni e Paolo in Venice. Its purpose is unclear, although it is inscribed with the little-known draughtsman's name and profession: 'Tomaso Belli Ingiegniero [Engineer]', which perhaps explains the complex and almost industrial nature of its composition. Both this and the previous drawing are contained within a volume of 36 measured drawings of Italian theatres, principally in the hand of the Italian architect, Carlo Fontana. This volume of drawings was among items purchased by Soane in 1818 at the Adam sale (see page 20).

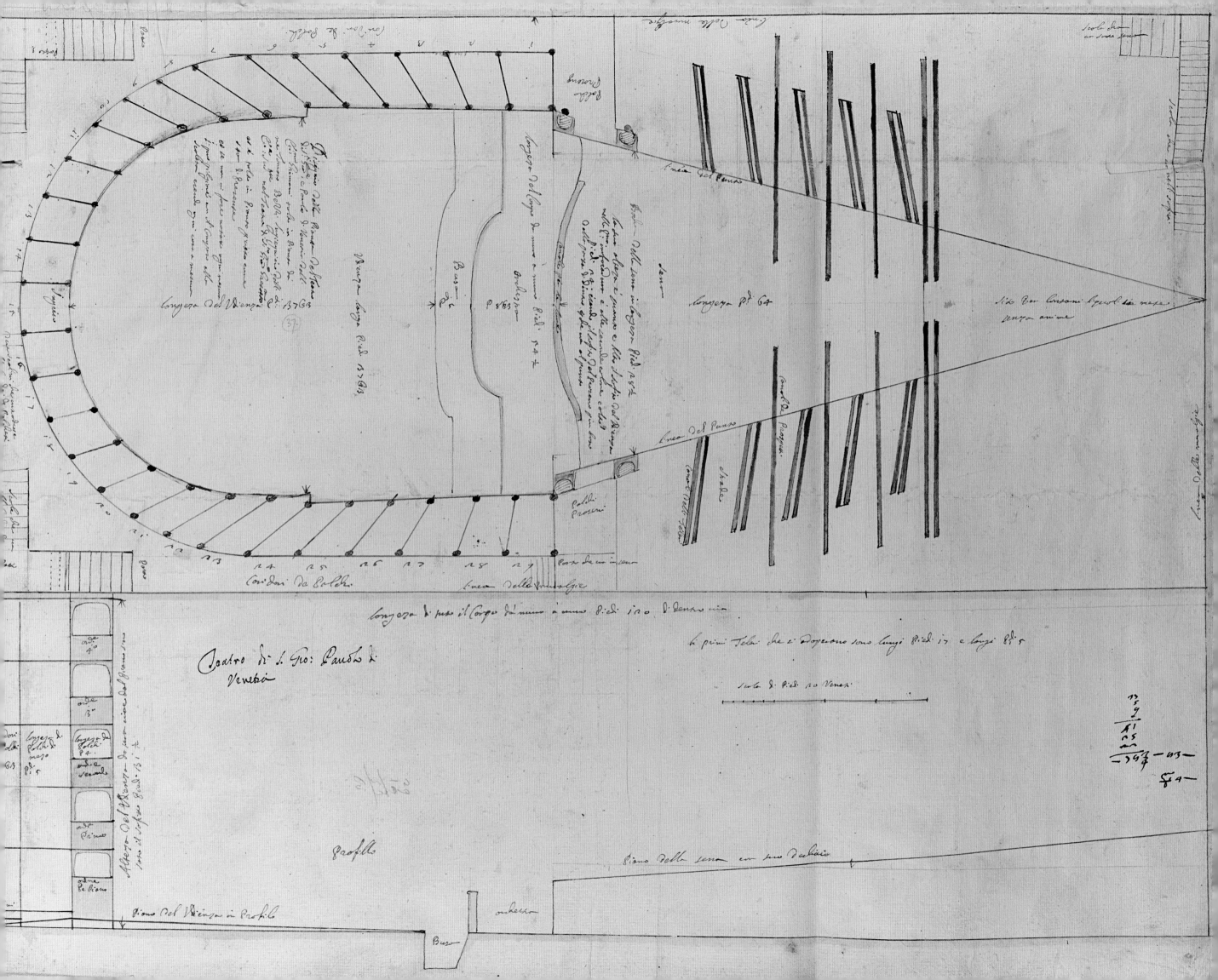

Teatro di S. Gio: Paolo di
Venetia

LAST FRONT PRACTICALLY AS CARRIED OUT.

●— **Nicholas Hawksmoor for Sir Christopher Wren, elevation of the east front of Hampton Court Palace, Richmond, 1689–90, SM volume 110/9. Photograph: Hugh Kelly.**

In 1689 King William III and Queen Mary II commissioned Sir Christopher Wren to make alterations to Hampton Court Palace. Wren was assisted in this great task by his clerk Nicholas Hawksmoor. This drawing, showing a design for the east front of Hampton Court facing the park, is one of a pair in Hawksmoor's hand: its sibling shows an elevation of the south front facing the Privy Garden. Although this is a highly finished presentation drawing, it dates from the early years of Wren's alterations and the arrangement shown above ground level does not correspond with the building as executed. The drawing is part of the now partly disbound *Hampton Court Album*, which contains the finest surviving drawings for William and Mary's works at Hampton Court. The volume flyleaf is signed by George Dance and annotated by Soane himself with the words 'to John Soane, Friday the 27th June 1817' indicating that it was a gift from Soane's former master and friend, the architect George Dance the Younger. How it came into Dance's ownership is not known, although it was sold to an unknown person at the sale of Wren's library and drawings collection of 1749.

Grinling Gibbons for Sir Christopher Wren, elevations of two chimneypieces and a frieze for Hampton Court Palace, Richmond, 1689–94, SM volume 110/23, 26, 62. Photographs: Hugh Kelly.

When King William III and Queen Mary II commissioned Sir Christopher Wren to make alterations to Hampton Court Palace in 1689, responsibility for the interiors was given to the famous English woodcarver Grinling Gibbons. There are 50 known surviving design drawings by Gibbons, 39 of which are held at the Soane Museum within a volume of designs for Hampton Court Palace (see page 43). Most of Gibbons's drawings contained in the volume are unexecuted designs for chimneypieces. The design, which includes a selection of pink ceramics, is of particular interest as it may indicate Gibbons

curating a display of items from Queen Mary's major collection of Japanese and Chinese porcelain. This had been held in the Queen's Gallery at Kensington Palace but was certainly moved – at least in part – to Hampton Court, as it was commented upon by the traveller Celia Fiennes during her visit in 1697. None of Gibbons's designs adhere to typical draughtsmanship practices of the time, for example, he seems to use colour to heighten the drama of the drawing rather than as a tool of accurate communication. Indeed, Gibbons was not a trained draughtsman, but his drawings offer an intense fluency and naturalism, and cleverly utilize shading to suggest contrast and three-dimensionality. Moreover, the designs are filled with ornamental motifs, which came to be typical of Gibbons's woodcarving, including cherubs, swags, fruit, trophies and strapwork.

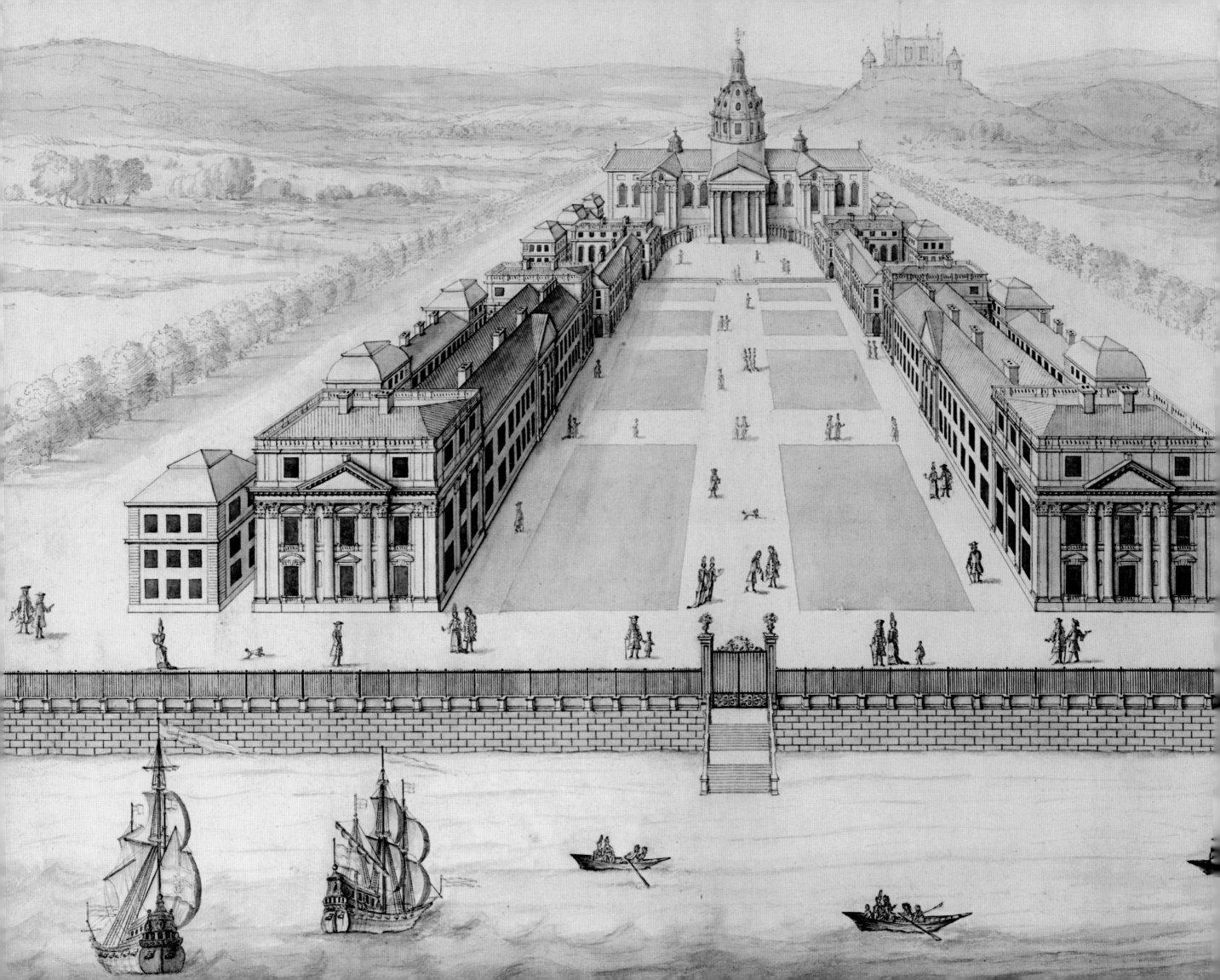

●— **Leonard Knyff for Sir Christopher Wren, bird's-eye view showing an unexecuted design for Greenwich Royal Hospital, Greenwich, 1694–5, SM volume 111/4. Photograph: Hugh Kelly.**
Leonard Knyff or Leendert Knijff was a Dutch draughtsman who is celebrated for his collaborative publication with Jan Kip entitled *Britannia Illustrata* (1707–9). The book offers bird's-eye perspective views of various significant country estates. At the time, the bird's-eye view was extremely innovative. This extraordinarily arresting presentation drawing predates the publication of *Britannia Illustrata* by at least 12 years and is probably one of the first bird's-eye view drawings made in Britain. It shows one of Sir Christopher Wren's earlier schemes for the construction of Greenwich Royal Hospital with a central domed hall and chapel range. Clearly Wren had relied on Knyff's conspicuous skill to beguile the Hospital Directors and persuade them to build the design. However, this ploy was unsuccessful as the central domed range completely obscures Inigo Jones's Queen's House beyond and thereby ignored the directors'

original brief to Wren that the view of the Queen's House should remain unimpeded. Indeed, a narrow strip of land between the Queen's House and the River Thames remained in the possession of the Crown in order to ensure this, and therefore could not be built upon by the hospital. It is amusing to note that Knyff has included the Royal Observatory in the background, albeit within an inaccurate landscape, which has either been improperly observed or is subject to artistic licence.

Although it is now disbound, this drawing comes from the *Christopher Wren and Inigo Jones Album*, containing 72 drawings for Hampton Court Palace and Greenwich Royal Hospital in a variety of hands. Eight of the drawings carry the collector's mark of William Talman, a friend and colleague of Sir Christopher Wren and it is probable that the volume was given or sold to Talman by Wren himself. The volume was listed in Soane's collection in 1831, but how and when it was acquired is not known.

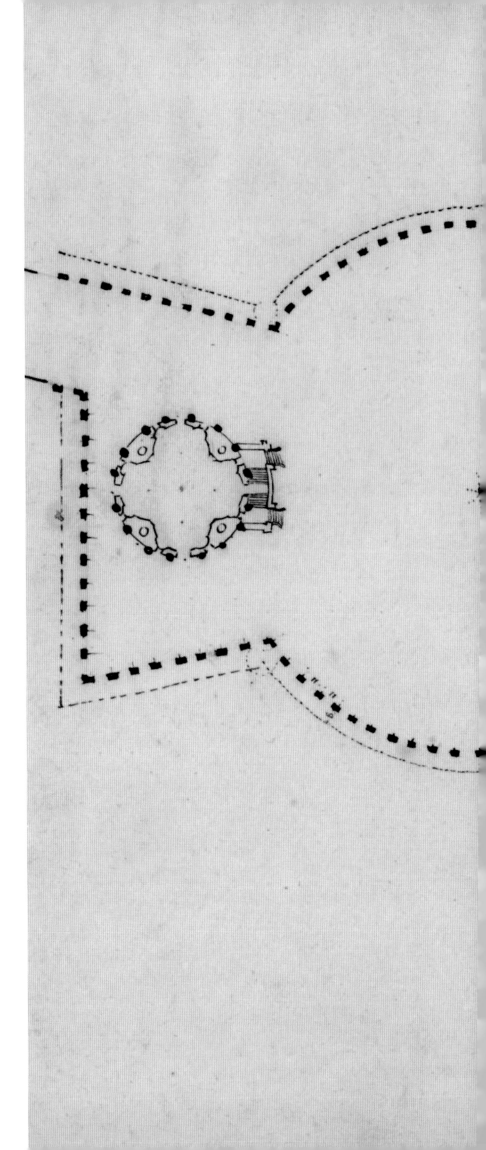

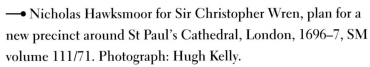 **Nicholas Hawksmoor for Sir Christopher Wren, plan for a new precinct around St Paul's Cathedral, London, 1696–7, SM volume 111/71. Photograph: Hugh Kelly.**

It is widely known that St Paul's Cathedral was rebuilt in 1675–1710 following the Great Fire of London to designs by Sir Christopher Wren with the assistance of his clerk Nicholas Hawksmoor. This is the only drawing in Soane's collection for St Paul's Cathedral that was made during its construction. It shows a plan of the Cathedral encircled by an unexecuted churchyard precinct, laid out like a piazza with arcaded frontages and with a rotunda to the west of the Cathedral. The rotunda has been variously described as a chapter house and a baptistry but was probably intended as a royal mausoleum. It has previously been observed that the precinct design was probably conceived by Hawksmoor himself but that the rotunda is heavily indebted to Wren's 1678 unexecuted scheme for a mausoleum to King Charles I at Windsor Castle. The inscription on the verso reads 'This drawing is in the hand of Sir Chris. Wren', but this misleading information is written in a later, eighteenth-century hand and the drawing has been firmly attributed to Hawksmoor on stylistic grounds. Like the previous drawing, this comes from the *Christopher Wren and Inigo Jones Album* (see page 47).

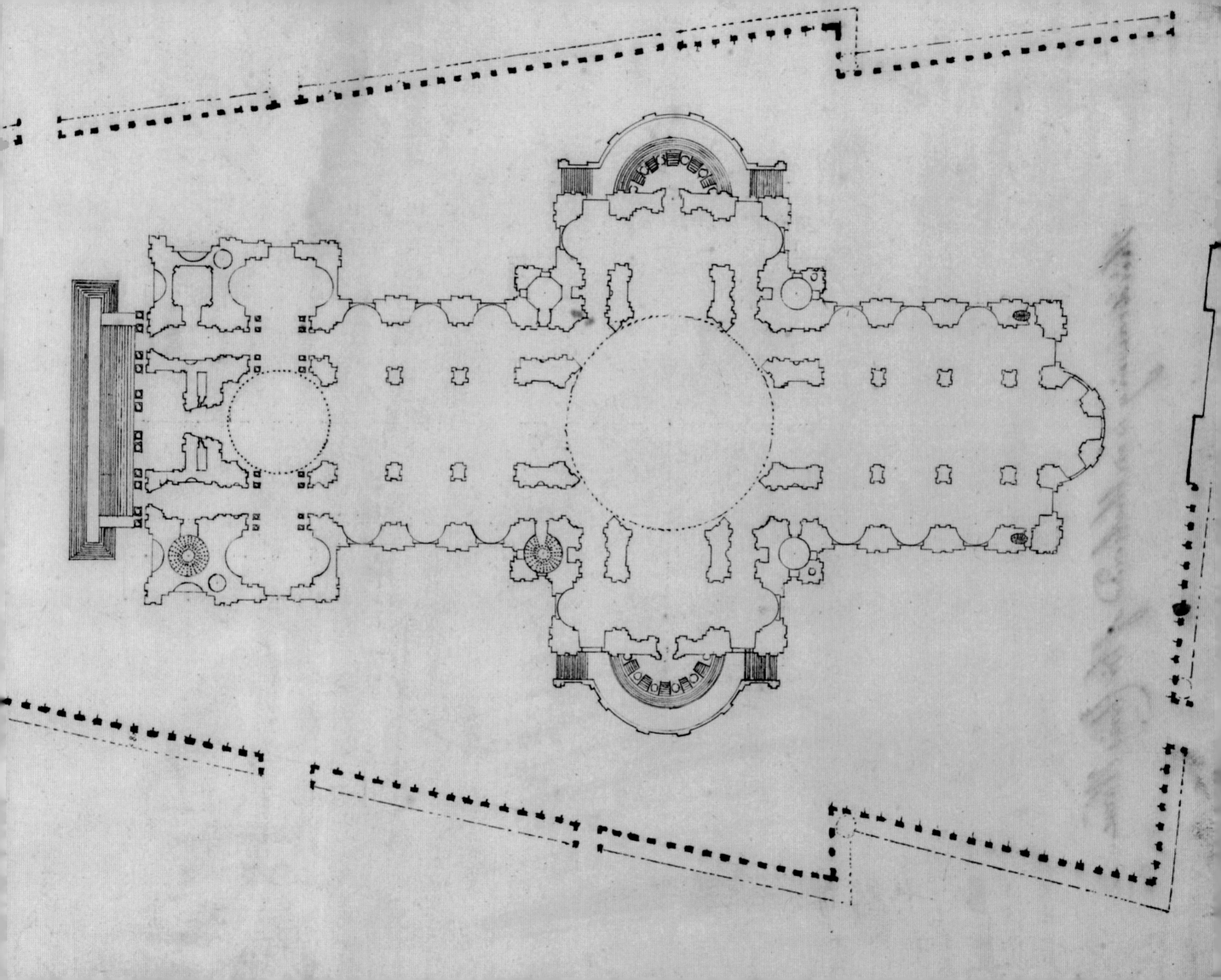

E. Section of y.e Temple with its new Imbellishments.

G. The fine Columns of Giallo Antico, And the Small altars or Tabernacles, having their Columns of porphyry

H. The Small pilasters over y.e great Columns, neither Answering to y.e Ribbs betwixt y.e pannels in the Shell of y.e Cupolo above them, nor the naked of the Columns below them.

I. The Attick kept plain, Much better than with y.e Small pilasters, having no proportion to y.e great Columns.

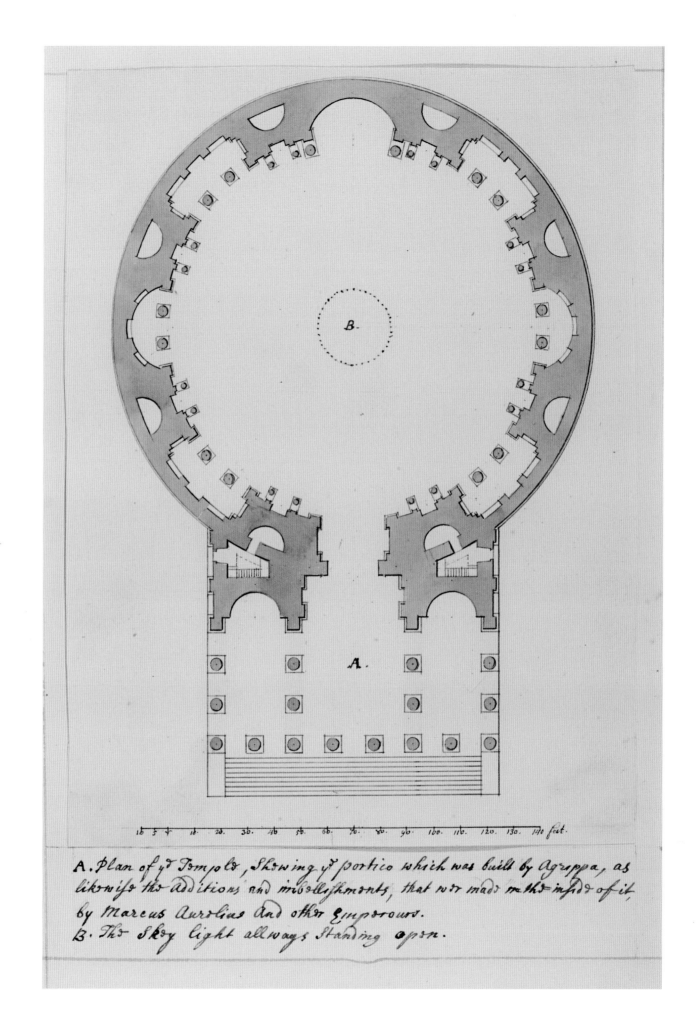

•→ **James Gibbs, plan and section of the Pantheon, Rome, 1707, SM volume 26/15, 17. Photographs: Hugh Kelly.**

These drawings of the Pantheon in Rome are contained within a small, leather-bound folio known as the *Gibbs Manuscript*, which includes sketches and notes apparently made in Italy in 1707 by the British architect James Gibbs. Gibbs described the folio as 'Memorandums for his own use', being a personal record or pattern book for reference once he had returned to England. However, recent scholarship has suggested that the contents of the folio were created as late as the 1750s, at the end of Gibbs's life, as the draft of a potentially profitable travel publication. These drawings were most probably made after drawings by the Italian architect Carlo Fontana, Gibbs's tutor during his time in Rome, showing the Pantheon and its eighteenth-century alterations. What became of the folio following Gibbs's death is unknown, but it is clear from a bill in the Soane Museum archives that it was purchased by Soane from the bookseller T. & W. Boone on 14 March 1826 for a meagre 16 shillings (SM Archives Spiers Box, Books purchased of T. Boone).

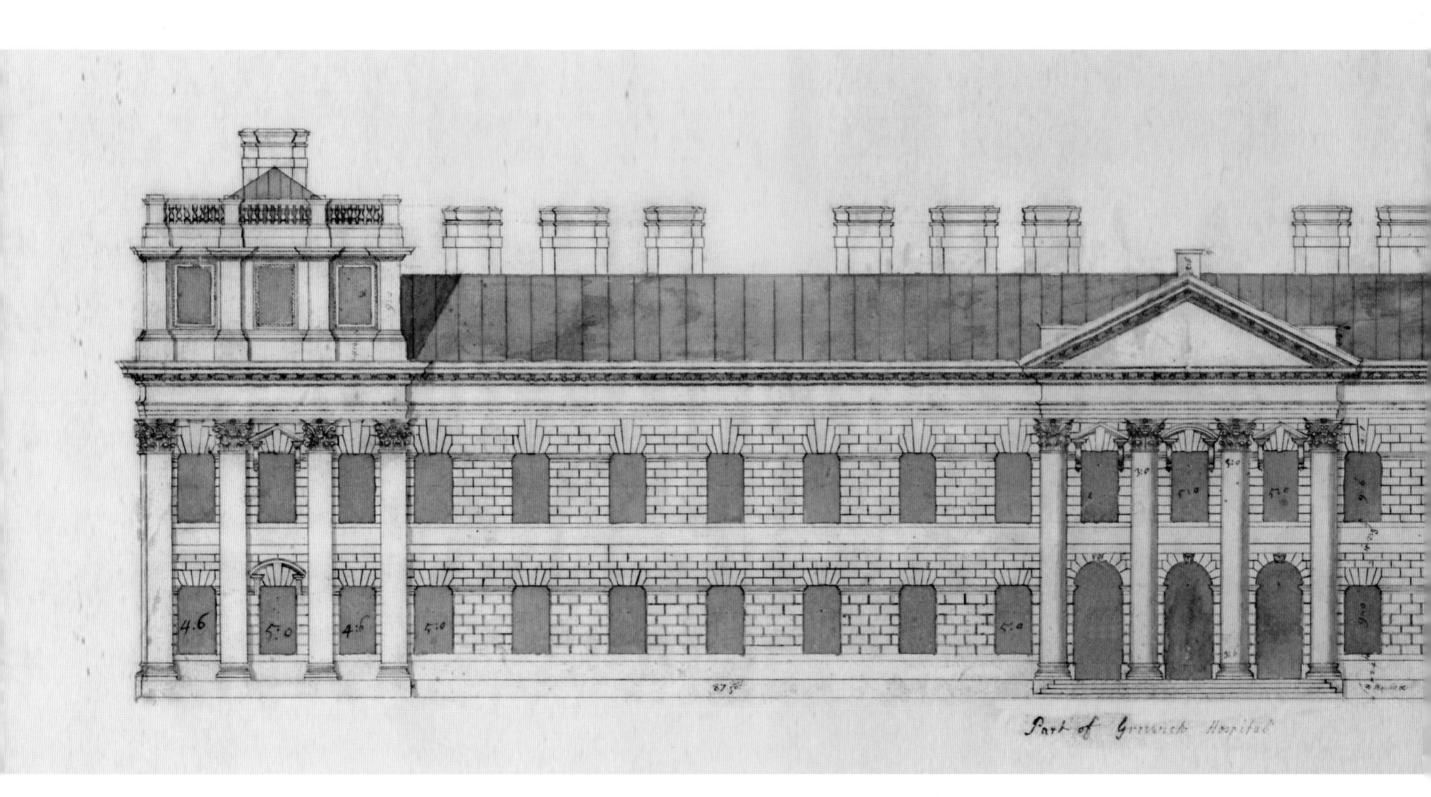

Part of Greenwich Hospital

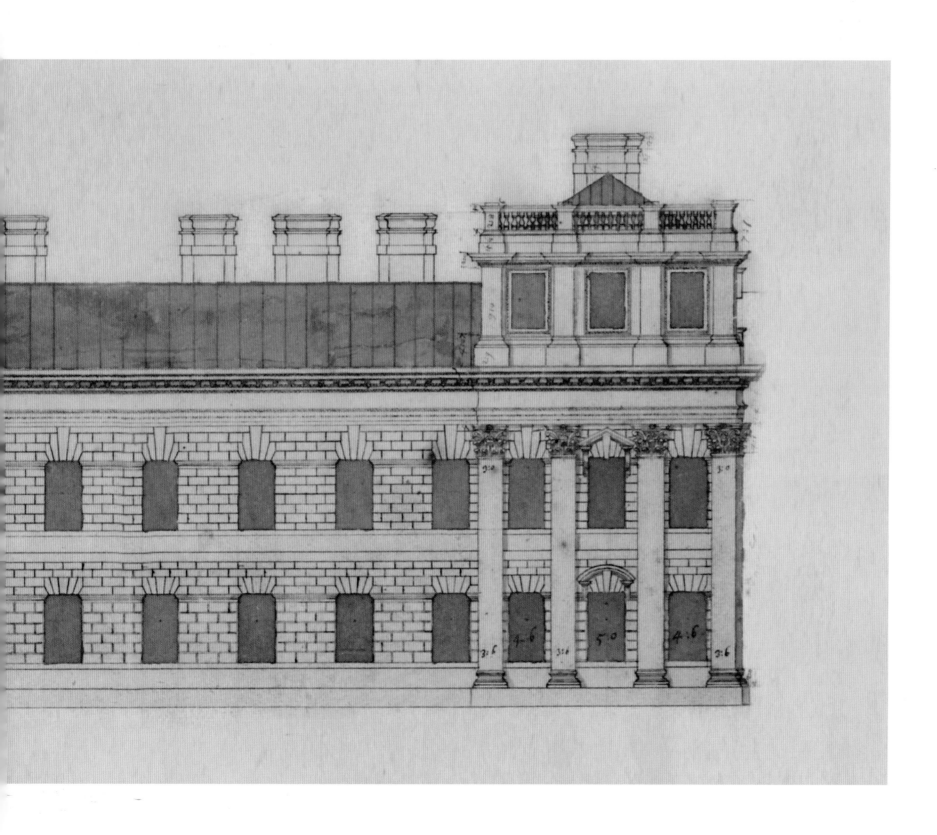

●— John James, east elevation of King Charles Court at Greenwich Royal Hospital, Greenwich, 1711–12, SM volume 111/9. Photograph: Hugh Kelly.

This drawing was previously attributed to the seventeenth-century architect John Webb (1611–72), who was responsible for designing the King Charles II Building at Greenwich Hospital. However, more recent scholarship has reattributed the drawing on account of the later style of draughtsmanship and given it to John James (c.1672–1746), who was co-Clerk of Works at Greenwich Hospital with Nicholas Hawksmoor and continued in this role after Hawksmoor's death in 1736. It is likely that James prepared the drawing in readiness for discussions between the Hospital Directors concerning the duplication of part of Webb's building in the Base Wing of the hospital. This is an excellent example of how difficult it can be to understand the authorship and history of individual drawings, particularly as it was included in the *Christopher Wren and Inigo Jones Album* (see page 47), alongside other drawings by Webb.

—• Sir James Thornhill, plan of a two-part painted ceiling,
*c.*1720–40, SM volume 111/55. Photograph: Hugh Kelly.
Specializing in large-scale history paintings, particularly murals in
the Baroque style, Sir James Thornhill is best remembered as the
artist who painted the dome of St Paul's Cathedral and the Painted
Hall at Greenwich Royal Hospital. He both designed and executed
his own work, which was in high demand. This drawing was once
contained in the *Christopher Wren and Inigo Jones Album* (see page
47). The volume comprised a series of Baroque designs, principally
for Hampton Court Palace and Greenwich Royal Hospital, but
this drawing is not thought to have been made for either of those
buildings. Although it is for an unknown place and subject, the
theatricality and three-dimensionality of the design is clear to see.

A Section of Noahs Ark.

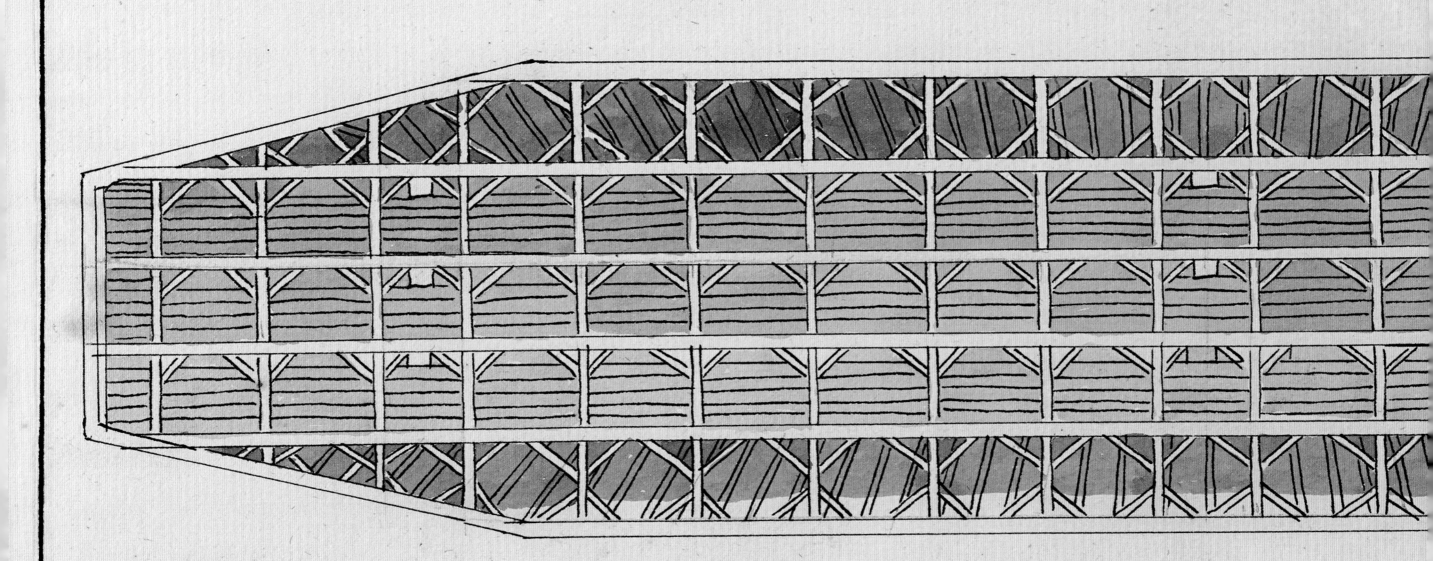

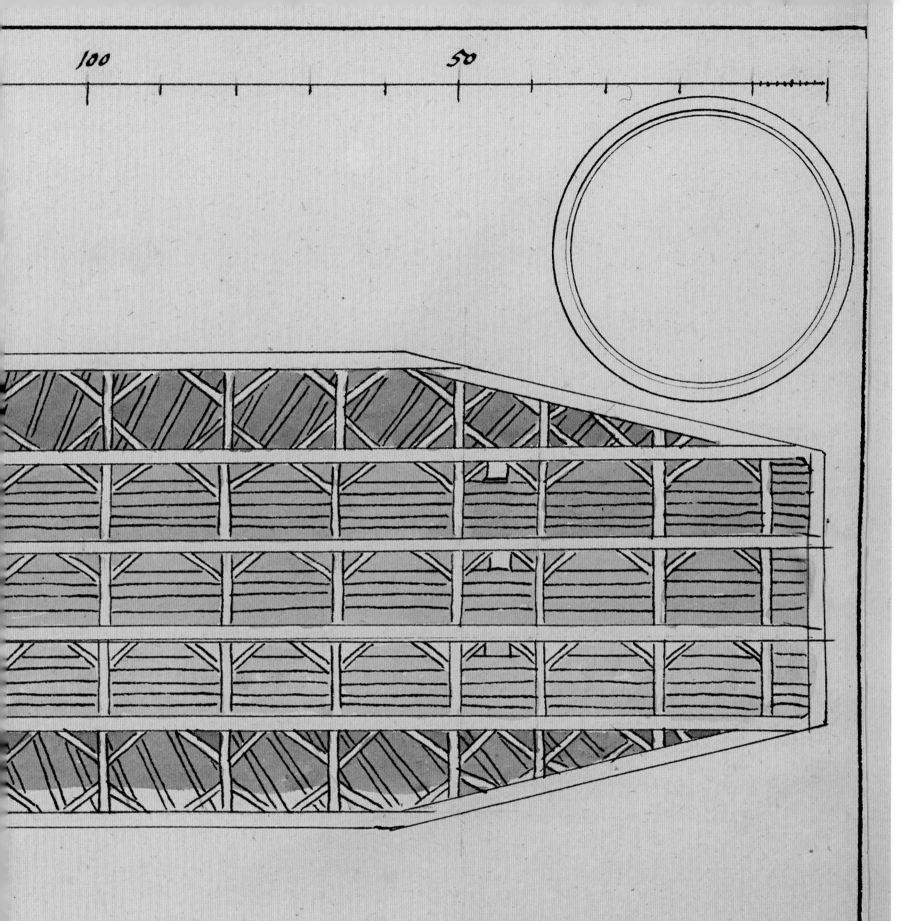

100   50

stukeley desig. 1735.

● — **William Stukeley, plan of Noah's Ark, 1735, SM volume 94/11. Photograph: Ardon Bar-Hama.**

This rather unusual plan of Noah's Ark, which later informed one of Soane's RA lecture drawings on the same subject, is found in one of four volumes containing drawings of sacred antiquities by William Stukeley (1687–1765). Stukeley was a clergyman of the Church of England, a physician and an antiquarian-cum-archaeologist. He published throughout his life and it is quite possible that this drawing was intended for that purpose. It was doubtless extrapolated from the description of Noah's Ark in the Bible:

Make thee an ark of gopher wood; rooms shalt thou make in the ark, and shalt pitch it within and without with pitch. And this is the fashion which thou shalt make it of: The length of the ark shall be three hundred cubits, the breadth of it fifty cubits, and the height of it thirty cubits. A window shalt thou make to the ark, and in a cubit shalt thou finish it above; and the door of the ark shalt thou set in the side thereof; with lower, second, and third stories shalt thou make it.
(Genesis 5:14–16.)

Soane purchased four volumes of Stukeley's drawings from the antiquarian John Britton on 14 January 1813 for £46.0.10 (SM Archives Journal 5, p.95).

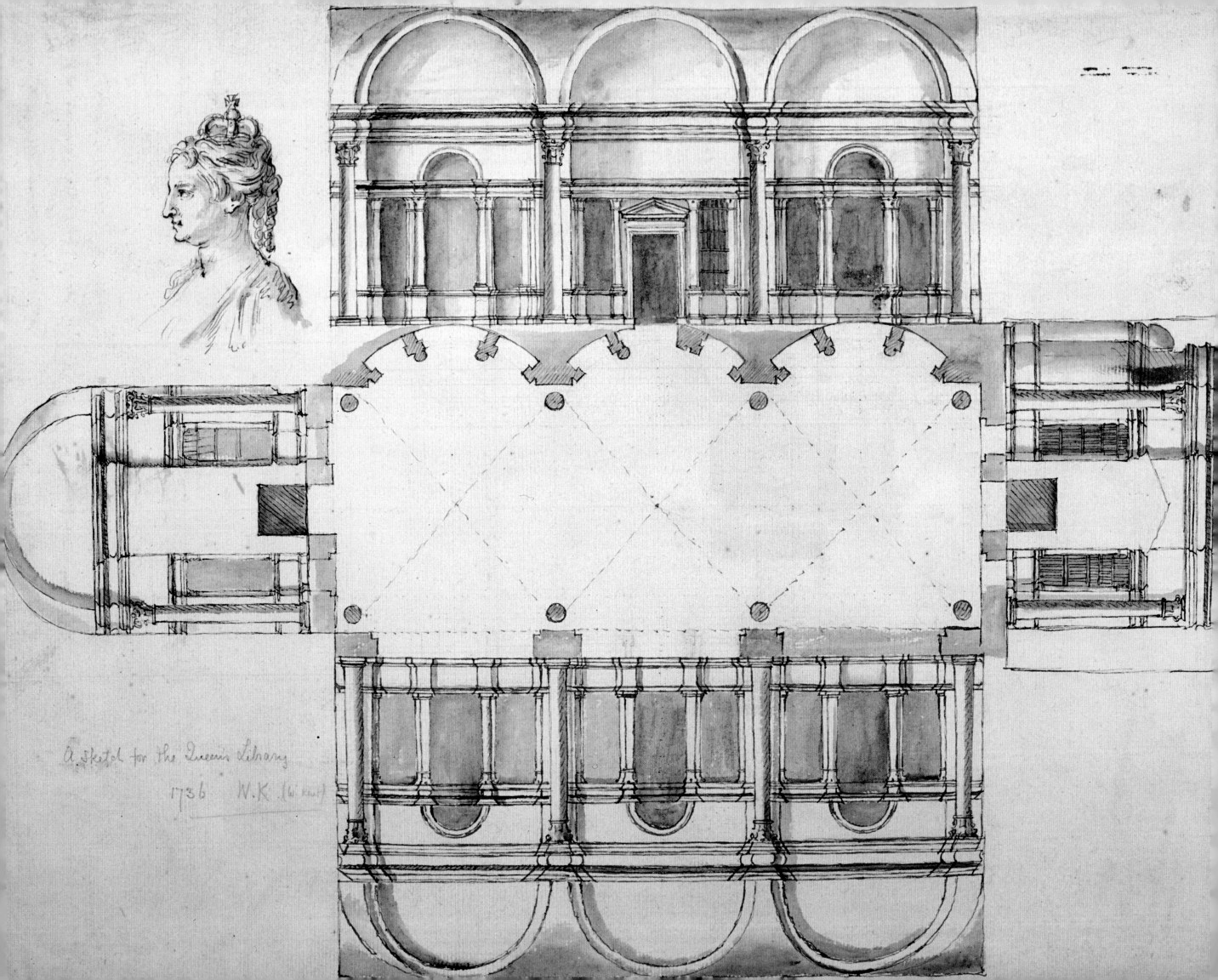

A Sketch for the Queen's Library
1736 W.K. (Wilkin)

●— **William Kent, laid-out wall elevations of Queen Caroline's library, St James's Palace, London, 1736–7, SM volume 147/197. Photograph: Geremy Butler.**

William Kent was a great favourite of Queen Caroline and from 1722 he received several commissions from the Royal family thanks to her influence. His last major Royal work was Queen Caroline's library at St James's Palace, completed in October 1737, just one month before her death. Here we see a charming vignette of Queen Caroline beside laid-out wall elevations for the library, which was composed of a single room within a block of 30 x 60ft (9 x 18m) overlooking Green Park. This is one of a number of drawings for the library in Soane's collection and appears to be one of the earliest in Kent's design sequence. It is found alongside numerous other drawings and prints within a grangerized series of Thomas Pennant's six-volume *Some Account of London* (1805). The Pennant volumes were previously in the possession of Henry Fauntleroy, a banker who was hanged for forgery in 1824. They were bought for 650 guineas by the antiquarian John Britton, who was acting as an agent for Soane at the sale of Fauntleroy's library at Sotheby's on 11 April 1825 (SM Archives Private Correspondence XVI.E.7.52).

➡— **William Kent, elevation and section of Queen Caroline's Hermitage, Richmond Gardens, Surrey, *c.*1730, Adam volume 56/33–34. Photograph: Hugh Kelly.**

| Charles-Louis Clérisseau, *capriccio*, *c*.1755–70, SM P68.
Photograph: Lewis Bush.

→ Jean-Baptiste Lallemand, view of the pyramid of Caius
Cestius, Rome, previously attributed to Charles-Louis Clérisseau,
1747–61, SM P109. Photograph: Geremy Butler.
Jean-Baptiste Lallemand was a French painter and draughtsman,
born in Dijon and trained in Paris but resident in Rome in 1747–61.
In 1755 he even worked as a landscape drawing tutor to Robert
Adam. This drawing must date from Lallemand's years in Rome as it
illustrates the iconic pyramid of Caius Cestius, built in *c*.18–12BCE
near the Porta Ostiensis. Adhering to the Roman craze for pyramids,
obelisks and sphinxes following the annexation of Egypt in 30BCE,
the pyramid was reputed to have been built in this form to prevent
Cestius's widow from dancing on his grave. It is not known how or
when this drawing came into Soane's collection. As it was previously,
wrongly, attributed to Lallemand's contemporary and countryman,
Charles-Louis Clérisseau, it is possible that Soane acquired it in
1796 along with others by Clérisseau, or that it had been included in
the Adam sale of 1818 (see page 20).

●— Sir William Chambers, view of a mausoleum for Frederick,
Prince of Wales, intended for Kew Gardens, Richmond, 1751, SM
17/7/11. Photograph: Geremy Butler.

Sir William Chambers was the son of a Scottish merchant born
in Gottenburg, Sweden. At 16 he joined the Swedish East India
Company, voyaging as far as Bengal and Canton (Guangzhou)
in China, and then in 1749, aged 27, he decided to focus on
architecture, spending a year at Blondel's École des Beaux-Arts in
Paris, followed in 1750 by five years in Italy. After this he settled in
London, quickly becoming successful and a favourite of the Royal
family. This design is thought to be a mausoleum for Frederick,
Prince of Wales, for Kew Gardens where Frederick's widow,
Augusta, Dowager Princess of Wales, would later commission
Chambers to build 25 garden buildings. Frederick had died in 1751,
four years before Chambers's return from Italy, so the mausoleum

design seems to be a grandiose speculative scheme produced while
Chambers was abroad, and probably intended for the perusal of
Augusta whom Chambers had met briefly in 1749. The design
has been described as the most splendid of Chambers's career
and was clearly inspired by the free-standing, centrally-planned
Roman mausolea such as those to Hadrian and Cecilia Metella.
This perspective drawing may have been produced for presentation
or perhaps even for exhibition, and it has been suggested that
Chambers's use of perspective and an idyllic landscape was
influenced by the teachings of the École des Beaux-Arts and the
pensionnaires of the French Academy in Rome. The design was
never executed, probably because such a scheme would have been
ruinously expensive to build. Soane acquired this drawing at the
Chambers sale of 1811 (see page 19).

—•Sir William Chambers and Laurent Pécheux, elevation of the Trevi Fountain, Rome, 1753, SM 22/2/8. Photograph: Ardon Bar-Hama.

The creation of this drawing was a collaboration between Sir William Chambers and the Rome-based French artist Laurent Pécheux, made during a five-year period when Chambers was studying in Italy. It illustrates Nicola Salvi's Trevi Fountain, which would later influence Chambers's greatest work at Somerset House in London. It has been suggested that the drawing was made from observation both of the fountain itself, and drawings from Salvi's office, as the statues flanking the central figure of Oceanus, as well as the reliefs above them, had not yet been executed. Soane

purchased this drawing at the Chambers sale of 1811 (see page 19). He clearly admired it enormously as he used it, alongside the work of his own office, to illustrate his lectures at the RA. He wrote of it:

I wish to call the attention of the student to the elevation of the Fontana di Trevi, as a drawing, which I regret is not in perspective. This drawing was made by the late Sir William Chambers whilst pursuing his studies in Italy. There is a chasteness in the manner and an effect produced without much labour which makes it more desirable to the architect than the present more elaborate mode of treating architectural design.
(Sir John Soane, RA lecture 5.)

A Perspective View of the MANSION HOUSE for the Residence of the Lord Mayor of the City of London for the time Being.
Finished in the Year 1753. and first Inhabited by Sʳ. CRISPE GASCOYNE. Kⁿᵗ. then Lord Mayor.

Architectura Georgii I

●— George Dance the Elder, view of the Mansion House, London, 1753, SM volume 17/1. Photograph: Ardon Bar-Hama.

George Dance the Elder was a mason-turned-architect who became Clerk of Works to the City of London in 1735. This appointment was doubtless influenced by his having won the commission to build the Mansion House, as a new residence for the Lord Mayor, a year earlier in 1734. Dance's drawings collection was inherited by his son, also an architect, George Dance the Younger, and the works of both father and son came into Soane's possession in 1836 when he purchased the entire collection for £500 (see page 21). This drawing is the most extraordinary from Dance the Elder's corpus. It is drawn on a splendid piece of vellum and is more highly finished than any of his other work. Moreover, it is drawn in perspective, from a vantage point which distorts reality, being located somewhere between Poultry and Princes Street in the middle of another building. It appears to be a fine presentation drawing, perhaps intended as a gift to Sir Crisp Gascoyne, the first Lord Mayor to take up residence. However, it has also been suggested that this is an elegant record drawing showing what Dance himself had hoped to achieve, produced when much of the building was already complete, but including unexecuted flourishes such as the figure of Justice surmounting the pediment, which Dance still hoped would come to fruition.

نور جهان بیکم

● — Unknown hand, plate from a volume of Indian and Persian miniatures and calligraphy, eighteenth century, SM volume 145/9. Photograph: Ardon Bar-Hama.

This charming Mughal miniature depicts a fine lady seated on a garden terrace while a maid combs her hair, and with another lady in the foreground playing a tambura. It is inscribed in Persian 'Nur Jahan Begum (Shah Jahan's wife)'. Shah Jahan (King of the World) was the fifth Mughal emperor who reigned in 1628–58. This drawing probably depicts Shah Jahan's favourite wife and Empress, Mumtaz Mahal (Chosen one of the Palace) with whom he had 14 children and on whose death he built the Taj Mahal in Agra. The miniature is found in a volume of eighteenth-century Indian and Persian miniatures, many of which carry the seal of Sir Elijah Impey, Chief Justice of Bengal in 1774–87, who compiled a large collection of miniatures that were sold at auction at H. Phillips of 73 Bond Street on 21 May 1810. The volume was presumably assembled a short time later. It was purchased by Soane for £21 from the sale of the newspaper proprietor James Perry's library in 1823.

━● George Dance the Younger, elevation of a detail of the entablature of the Temple of Vesta, Tivoli, *c.*1762, SM D3/1/6. Photograph: Ardon Bar-Hama.

Thanks to the professional success of his mason-cum-architect father, George Dance the Younger was able to undertake a Grand Tour in 1759–64 and study the classical tradition of architecture in Italy. This accomplished and highly finished record drawing dates from that time and shows the Corinthian entablature of the Temple of Vesta at Tivoli, ornamented with ox skulls and festoons. Such drawings were made by architects when on their Grand Tour, both as a means of familiarizing themselves with specific motifs and in order to document the forms for future reference. John Soane was doubtless inspired by such drawings during his time as Dance's apprentice from 1768. In fact, there is a close copy of this drawing on display at the Soane Museum, albeit omitting Dance's name, which had been made by Soane in 1779, suggesting that Soane had borrowed Dance's drawing long before it came into his possession along with the wider Dance collection in 1836 (see page 21). The Temple of Vesta at Tivoli was Soane's favourite building and inspired a number of his works including the famous Tivoli Corner at the Bank of England.

O · LL GELLIO · L F

E OF A TEMPLE AT TIVOLI.

E OF ENGLISH FEET.   G DANCE. ARCH.

●— **Office of George Dance the Younger, bird's-eye view of Newgate Gaol, contract design, 1769–70s, SM D4/4/16. Photograph: Geremy Butler.**

In 1768 George Dance the Elder resigned his position as Clerk of Works to the City of London in favour of his son, and George Dance the Younger's first major commission in that capacity was to rebuild Newgate Gaol. It became his most celebrated masterpiece, being an imposing, rugged building, not unlike the Baroque work of John Vanbrugh from half a century earlier, and eminently suited to its use. Charles Dickens described the entrances at Newgate Gaol as 'looking as if they were made for the express purpose of letting people in, and never letting them out again'. This bird's-eye view presentation drawing demonstrates the arrangement of three enclosed quadrangles, dividing the inmates by men, women and debtors. It shows the façade and central Governor's House as they were executed, with the exception of the four statues within aedicules, which might have been executed but are not visible in photographs taken before Newgate Gaol's demolition in 1902. Jill Lever suggested that Dance's design may have been inspired by Giovanni Battista Piranesi's *Carceri d'Invenzione* (1749) series of fantasy prison designs, although the style of draughtsmanship here could not be more different to that of Piranesi, being scrupulously accurate and austere. There are three Dance office drawings for the exterior of Newgate Gaol in Soane's collection, all acquired when Soane purchased the Dance collection in 1836 (see page 21), and as Dance required such a high standard from his draughtsmen all three show exactly the same arrangement right down to the number of stone courses. Soane had been apprenticed to Dance from 1768 and remained his close friend until Dance's death in 1825, albeit with occasional fallings-out, so it is heartening to know that following his return from the Grand Tour, when Soane was sorely in need of work, Dance employed him to draw up estimates for Newgate Gaol.

●— Charles Cameron, plan of a ceiling for the dining parlour at 15 Hanover Square, London, 1770–5, SM 44/9/15. Photograph: Geremy Butler.

The Scottish architect Charles Cameron trained under Isaac Ware (1704–66) and undertook a visit to Rome in 1768–9. He worked in a Roman-inspired Neo-classical style similar to that of Robert Adam, and in 1778 he departed for Russia, where he served as court architect to the great anglophile Empress Catherine the Great. He maintained this position until Catherine's death in 1796, apparently remaining in Russia until his own death in 1812, working on projects in and around St Petersburg, including major additions to the Pavlovsk Palace and the Catherine Palace at Tsarskoe Selo. During the 1770s in London, between his time in Italy and Russia, Cameron had busied himself with publication projects. The only evidence of him working as an architect during that time relates to the construction of 15 Hanover Square, London, for Jervoise Clarke. Cameron is listed as the architect of that house in a series of bills now held in the Hampshire Record Office. His role there was perhaps due to his father, Walter Cameron, who was the executant carpenter in 1770–4. This ceiling design, which is signed by Cameron, was almost certainly made for the same house. Drawings by Cameron from his years in England are extremely rare and how this sheet came into Soane's collection is not known.

➡• Charles Cameron, elevations and sections of the Baths of Diocletian, Rome, thought to have been made in preparation for Cameron's publication of *The Baths of the Romans* in 1772, SM 44/7/7. Photograph: Hugh Kelly.

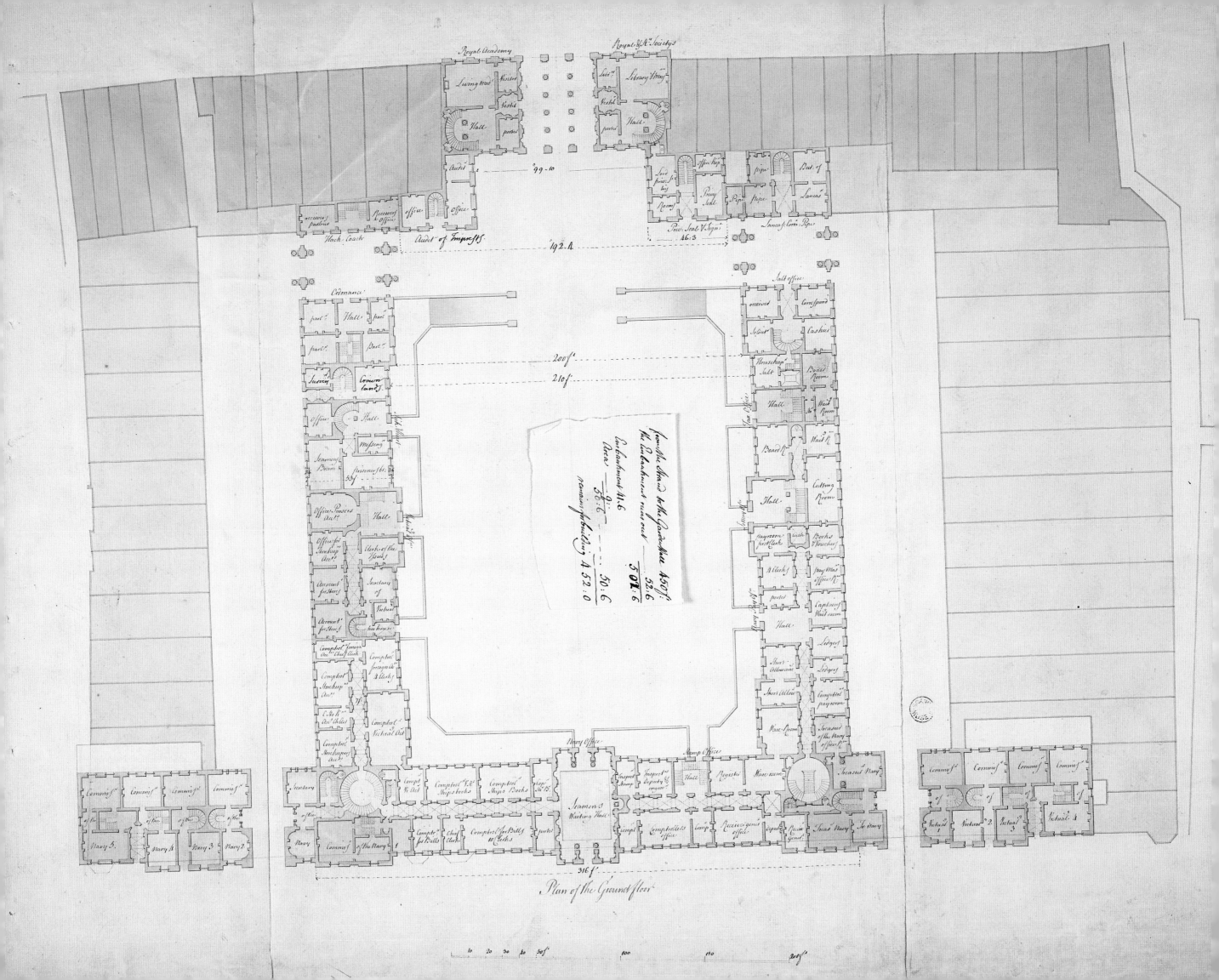

Plan of the Ground floor

●—— **Office of Sir William Chambers, plan of Somerset House, and elevation of a detail for the façade of Somerset House, Strand, London, *c*.1775–90, SM 41/1/18, SM 42/1/27. Photographs: Ardon Bar-Hama and Geremy Butler.**

Somerset House on the north bank of the River Thames was originally constructed for Lord Protector Somerset from 1547. Thereafter it functioned variously for Royal use and as grace and favour apartments, being much altered over the years and falling into disrepair during the eighteenth century. The rebuilding of Somerset House from 1775, facilitating the centralization of government, constituted one of the largest and most prominent public architectural commissions in eighteenth-century London. Considering Chambers's popularity with King George III it is perhaps unsurprising that he was chosen to make the designs. His arrangement recalls the Neo-classical urban architecture of Paris, appearing from the exterior to comprise a single large building, but being divided internally into individual units, all clustered around a courtyard. This plan does not show Somerset House exactly as executed, but note the subtle use of coloured wash to indicate the various quarters assigned to different organizations. Moreover, it can be seen here that Chambers always intended a grandiose tripartite portal between the Strand and the courtyard in the northern range, and an awe-inspiring southern façade facing the river.

The drawing of a detail of the façade shows one bay in the central portion of the south, east and west ranges, albeit in execution with an arched window on the ground storey rather than a pedimented one within a relieving arch. Moreover, a number of the ornamental details were omitted in execution, such as the ground-storey mask keystone, the first-storey relief panel above the window and the second-storey mask and swags above the window. Furthermore, the order of the capitals is Composite as executed rather than Corinthian as shown here. Other features, however, adhere closely to the drawing, for example the rhythm of the fenestration and the form of the rustication, balustrade and modillions. The omission of ornamental details in execution was presumably made in an effort to economize. Despite this, upon completion the building had cost an eye-watering half a million pounds of public money. The large scale and exceptional quality of this drawing suggest that it was produced for exhibition and illustrates the calibre of the draughtsmen of the Chambers office.

There are almost seven hundred Chambers office drawings for Somerset House in Soane's collection. We know that these were sold along with Chambers's other possessions in 1811, but they were not purchased by Soane at that time, and it is not known when they came into his collection (see page 19).

SKETCH OF THE LIBRARY, LANSDOWN

VSE .

●— **Office of George Dance the Younger, section through a library for Lansdowne House, Berkeley Square, London, 1788–94, SM D3/3/5. Photograph: Ardon Bar-Hama.**

Lansdowne House had been built from 1760 to designs by Robert Adam for the politician and bibliophile Lord Bute. Adam included a large library wing at the rear of the house for Bute's famously extensive collection of books. However, following Bute's retirement, he sold the house in 1765 to the 1st Marquess Lansdowne who was more interested in antique sculpture than books, and so began half a century of indecision about whether the rear wing should be fitted up as a library or as a sculpture gallery. After Adam's time, four other architects were consulted about the wing before George Dance's scheme for a library, as seen here, was finally executed in 1788–91, only to be demolished when the space was transformed into a Greek Revival-style sculpture gallery in 1816–19 to designs by Robert Smirke (1780–1867). Although it was short-lived, Dance's richly frescoed library was extremely fine, being modelled on the Roman interiors then being excavated at Pompeii. This drawing was acquired by Soane in 1836 when he purchased the entire Dance drawings collection for £500 (see page 21).

●— **Humphry Repton, perspective view with a flier from the Red Book for the park at Wood Hill House, Hertfordshire, 1803, SM volume 30/9b. Photograph: Ardon Bar-Hama.**

Humphry Repton described himself as a 'landscape gardener' and he worked in the naturalistic style of Lancelot 'Capability' Brown (*c*.1715–83), albeit often paying more attention to the immediate surroundings of a house – the garden – rather than the wider landscape. Less prolific than Brown in his executed works, Repton is probably best known for his publications on gardening and the Red Books he made for each client, so-called as they comprised a volume of designs and explanations for improvements, bound in red Moroccan leather. Of particular note was Repton's use of fliers or flaps in the Red Books, allowing the reader to see drawn views of the landscape both before and after the proposed changes. Only around a hundred of Repton's Red Books survive. This example is in particularly good condition, but it is not known how it came into Soane's collection. It contains eight pages of explanatory text and five drawings – four with flaps – proposing alterations at Wood Hill, such as masking the stables from the road with trees, the erection of boundary fencing and the attractive additions of trellis and planting to the exterior of the house. Unfortunately, we do not know if any of this work ever came to fruition as the house was demolished in 1820.

THE ADAM DRAWINGS COLLECTION

There are around 9,000 drawings within the Adam collection at the Soane Museum, comprising over 80 per cent of the surviving Adam drawings in the world. Various sheets were acquired by Soane in 1818 at the Christie's sale of Robert and James Adam's artworks and library, but the vast majority came to Soane in 1833 when he purchased the bulk of the Adam office drawings from Robert and James Adam's niece, Susannah Clerk (see page 20).

Robert Adam, *capriccio* of the interior of a barrel-vaulted hall, *c.*1756–57, SM Adam volume 56/132. Photograph: Hugh Kelly.

●— Giovanni Battista Piranesi, *capriccio*, 1745–50, SM Adam volume 56/146. Photograph: Hugh Kelly.

Owing to a series of well-known publications, the Italian designer Giovanni Battista Piranesi was one of the most influential artists of the eighteenth century. Robert Adam first met Piranesi in Rome at the start of his Grand Tour in June 1755. On 4 July 1755 Robert wrote to his family in Scotland: 'so amazing and ingenious fancies as he [Piranesi] has produced in the different plans of the Temples, Baths and Palaces and other buildings I never saw and are the greatest fund for inspiring and instilling invention in any lover of architecture that can be imagined … whatsoever I want of him he will do for me with pleasure, and is just now doing two drawings for me which will both be singular and clever'. Adam returned to London in 1758 with the two aforementioned drawings by Piranesi among his souvenirs; this *capriccio* is one of them. It is particularly significant for its similarity to Piranesi's famous *Carceri d'Invenzione* (1749) series of fantasy prison designs, drawn in pen, wash and chalk. The Neo-classical Adam style, that infused houses across Britain and later, in the nineteenth century, also America, was in no small part stimulated by the fulsome – almost chaotic – details and stylistic synthesis found in Piranesi's work.

Giovanni Battista Piranesi, unfinished *capriccio* of funerary monuments, being the second drawing given by Piranesi to Robert Adam during his Grand Tour, *c.*1755, SM Adam volume 26/163. Photograph: Hugh Kelly.

—— Robert Adam, *capriccio*, 1756–7, SM Adam volume 56/104. Photograph: Hugh Kelly.

This sketch-like but realistic *capriccio* of a sarcophagus and other fragments in front of a curved arcade is typical of Robert Adam's new-found Grand Tour drawing style thanks to the tutelage of Charles-Louis Clérisseau, Laurent Pécheux and others. This was cultivated during his time living at the Casa Guarnieri near the Spanish Steps in Rome. Clérisseau's teaching style evidently involved his pupil emulating his own work, and there are numerous examples of pairs of drawings by Clérisseau and Adam, which illustrate the same subject matter depicted in the same medium. This drawing in pencil, pen and watercolour is in Adam's own hand and is comparable with one by Clérisseau of around the same date, also in pencil, pen and watercolour, and also depicting a sarcophagus and other fragments in front of a curved arcade, albeit with part of a coffered dome rather than the elaborate sculptural frieze seen in Adam's version here. Even Adam's use of pink-purple wash, indicating that the imaginary sarcophagus is made of precious porphyry, was copied from the drawing by Clérisseau.

→•Antonio Zucchi for James Adam, elevation of the Britannic capital for Adam's unexecuted Parliament House, 1762, SM Adam volume 7/69. Photograph: Hugh Kelly.

During the winters of 1762 and 1763, on his Grand Tour, James Adam set about designing a new Parliament House, which he hoped would be built in London through the good graces of the politician, the Earl of Bute, who was a favourite of King George III. Despite tuition from Charles-Louis Clérisseau, James lacked his brother Robert's talent for drawing and the majority of his Parliament House designs were redrawn as presentation drawings by the Venetian artist Antonio Zucchi who was then working for him as a draughtsman. There are over a hundred surviving drawings for James's Parliament House, and this is by far the most alluring. This so-called Britannic capital is ornamented with a collection of British motifs: a lion, unicorn, crown, sceptre, thistle, roses and the collar of the Order of the Garter. It was intended for the principal portico of Parliament House while the drawing itself was made for presentation to King George III via Lord Bute. James described the drawing as follows:

This British order invented in Rome by J. A. Archt. & intended for the principal portico of a parliament house design'd by him at Rome 1762 most humbly presented to H.M. The King by his subject & servt the Author.

Although James's Parliament House was never built, the Adam brothers cleverly recycled the Britannic capital, using it on the design for the pilasters adorning the entrance screen to Carlton House on Pall Mall for Augusta, Dowager Princess of Wales, in 1767. According to the first volume of the brothers' *Works in Architecture of Robert and James Adam* (1773–8), the design was much favoured by Augusta, and would have been executed but for her declining health.

●—— **Agostino Brunias for Robert Adam, view made for publication showing the Admiralty Screen on Whitehall, London, 1759, SM Adam volume 35/4. Photograph: Ardon Bar-Hama.**

In 1759, the Lords of the Admiralty agreed to sell a portion of their forecourt for £650 to the Westminster Bridge Commissioners for a street-widening scheme. The original boundary wall, contemporary with Thomas Ripley's Admiralty building of 1723–6, was demolished and a new screen wall was commissioned from Robert Adam. Although Adam had only returned from his Grand Tour in December 1758 – bringing the talented Roman painter and draughtsman Agostino Brunias (*c*.1730–96) with him – Adam is thought to have received this prominent commission thanks to the influence of two Lords of the Admiralty: his neighbour from Kinross-shire Sir Gilbert Elliott of Minto, and the Rt Hon. Edward Boscawen for whom he was already decorating the interiors at

Hatchlands in Surrey. The refined 140ft (43m) screen wall appears to be loosely based on the Arch of Titus in Rome, but at the time of its construction its rhythmical Neo-classical forms were conspicuously *nouveau* compared to the neo-Palladian architecture of the preceding years.

Adam himself commissioned Brunias to produce this captivating perspective view of the Admiralty Screen in order that it might be engraved. The sheet has been folded four times, most likely when it was sent to the engraver. Adam was prodigiously proud of this first public commission in London and wanted to publicize the work. The engraving was published in February 1761 for sale in the bookshop of Andrew Millar on the Strand for 2s 6d, along with an elevation and plan showing the Admiralty Screen as built. It was also included in the first volume of *The Works in Architecture of Robert and James Adam* (1773–8).

→•**Attributed to Agostino Brunias for Robert Adam, section through the hall and salon at Kedleston Hall, Derbyshire, 1760, SM Adam volume 40/3. Photograph: Geremy Butler.**

The single most magnificent series of presentation drawings in the Adam collection at the Soane Museum was made in 1760 for Sir Nathaniel Curzon, 5th Baronet, the owner of Kedleston Hall in Derbyshire. These comprise three large-scale plans for the different storeys; elevations of the north and south fronts which are over 6½ft (2m) long; and a pair of intricate sectional drawings, one longitudinal and the other axial, offering a view of the interior. This is the axial section from that group, cutting through the central mass of the building and offering a glimpse of the two principal rooms: the marble hall and saloon. The building was executed with only minor alterations to this design. The Curzon family have lived at Kedleston since the thirteenth century, but Adam's patron, Sir Nathaniel, had inherited a red-brick Queen Anne house of *c.*1700 by Francis Smith of Warwick (1672–1738). Upon deciding to rebuild in 1758 there was some indecision as to the best architect. First to be employed was Matthew Brettingham (1699–1769) and then James Paine (1717–89), both of whom managed to build a single pavilion before being replaced. It was doubtless owing to this professional opposition that Adam felt inclined to provide such elaborate drawings. Happily, they were fine enough to lure Sir Nathaniel away from these competitors and Adam took control of the house by the end of April 1761. His design for the central block at Kedleston was required to fit between the pre-existing Brettingham and Paine pavilions but this did not prevent Adam from designing on a majestic scale. Here we see the two central rooms arranged as a Roman atrium and vestibulum taken from the reconstruction of Pliny's Villa Laurentinum in *Villas of the Ancients* by Robert Castell (1728). The circular saloon is reminiscent of the Pantheon, while the marble hall is lined with sculpture-filled niches and ornamented with column capitals inspired by the Temple of Jupiter Stator as published in Andrea Palladio's *I quattro libri dell'architecttura* (1570). This was eighteenth-century antiquarian architecture at its best.

Front of a Bracket for a Clock for His Majesty.

➤ Robert Adam, elevation of a clock bracket for George III at Buckingham House, London, 1761–3, and, attributed to Joseph Bonomi for Robert and James Adam, plan, elevation and section of door furniture for Syon Park, Brentford, 1767–8, SM Adam volume 25/20, 49. Photographs: Ardon Bar-Hama.

For those patrons who could afford it, Robert Adam offered an all-inclusive service, ranging from the foundations of the building to the tableware. These two designs exemplify his ability to design exceptional metalwork items for his interiors. However, such items were rarely executed owing to the expense of bespoke pieces compared with those that were readily available to all.

Following George III's purchase of Buckingham House in 1762, it was subject to considerable alterations and Adam was responsible for a small number of additions to the interior. This design for a rather frivolous gilded clock bracket is suitably ornamented with the royal insignia of a lion and unicorn but was never executed.

Originally a Bridgettine monastery built from 1431, Syon Park was modernized with elaborate Adam interiors in the 1760s for the 1st Duke and Duchess of Northumberland. There is no evidence that this scheme for the door furniture was ever used – the Duke was vastly wealthy but also shrewd; instead the design was reused at nearby Osterley Park for the *nouveau riche* banker Robert Child.

●— **Giuseppe Manocchi for Robert and James Adam, plan of a carpet, 1765–6, SM Adam volume 15/3. Photograph: Ardon Bar-Hama.**

During his Grand Tour of 1761–3, James Adam commissioned the gifted Roman draughtsman Giuseppe Manocchi to make studies of Italian architecture and 86 of these drawings survive in Soane's collection. However, it was following Manocchi's move to the Adam office in London in 1765, that the majority of his drawings for the brothers were made. Although he contributed heavily to the daily output of drawings for clients, this drawing is one of a group of 166 for which there appears to have been no particular patron, and which were never executed. Rather, these were ornamental schemes offering inspiration for the motifs and colours of grotesque panels, ceilings and carpets. Some emulated the unpublished drawings of Pietro and Francesco Santi Bartoli held in the library at Eton College, and others were influenced by Manocchi's memories of Raphael's loggia at the Vatican. They utilize a vibrant palette of colours, often further emboldened by the application of gouache rather than standard watercolour. It is generally agreed that Manocchi's principal influence on the Adam style was this rich use of colour, and from the mid-1760s onwards, there was a corresponding shift in the Adam brothers' designs towards Manocchi's bold colourways. Four payments totalling £134 were made to Manocchi from the Adam brothers' Drummonds Bank account in 1765–6. This is a far greater sum than the standard salary of a draughtsman – even one as talented as Manocchi – and it is assumed that this money provided remuneration for his 166 inspirational drawings.

→● Giuseppe Manocchi for Robert and James Adam, plan of a ceiling for the circular dressing room at Harewood House, West Yorkshire, 1767, SM Adam volume 11/148. Photograph: Ardon Bar-Hama.

This extraordinarily handsome drawing is perhaps the best example of why Giuseppe Manocchi was employed as a master draughtsman in the Adam office for eight years. The Roman draughtsman's talents were prodigious, and here we can see that his foliate and figurative motifs were particularly impressive, with garlands and nymphs encircling a band of grotesque work around the face of Apollo. The drawing offers one of two schemes designed for the domed ceiling of the circular dressing room – one of two dressing rooms adjoining the state bedchamber – at Harewood House in Yorkshire. The Harewood estate had been in the possession of the sugar-trading Lascelles family since 1739, and the original seventeenth-century house was rebuilt by Edwin Lascelles, Baron Harewood, from 1759. Adam initially worked at Harewood in collaboration with John Carr of York, a local master mason-cum-architect and distant relative of the Lascelles family, but from the autumn of 1765, once the architectural shell was complete, Adam was given sole responsibility for the interior decoration. Harewood was the largest country house project of Adam's career and provided employment for him until 1782. Unfortunately, this sumptuous design never came to fruition and instead a simpler plasterwork scheme was designed by Adam and executed by the *stuccadore* Joseph Rose (1744–99), who charged £125 for his work in the room. This was demolished in favour of a corridor in the 1840s when Sir Charles Barry (1795–1860) was commissioned to remodel and modernize the house.

Cieling of the Library at Kenwood in Middlesex.

●— Attributed to William Hamilton for Robert and James Adam, plan of the library ceiling for Kenwood House, Hampstead, 1767, SM Adam volume 11/112. Photograph: Ardon Bar-Hama.

It is perhaps surprising that this library, one of Adam's finest surviving rooms, should be found in a small suburban villa such as Kenwood. The house has Jacobean roots but was largely rebuilt in the 1690s and an orangery wing was added in *c.*1750. It was purchased in 1754 by the Hon. William Murray, Lord Chief Justice and later 1st Earl of Mansfield. Having decided to regularize the house by building a library wing to mirror the orangery, Murray approached the Adam brothers to make designs. In fact, James's unexecuted designs for the Kenwood library launched his London career in 1764. However, it was Robert's scheme, the ceiling for which can be seen here, which was executed three years later. The ceiling is of the highest quality with plasterwork by the *stuccadore* Joseph Rose and mythologically-themed medallions painted by Antonio Zucchi. Now in the stewardship of English Heritage, Kenwood has recently been subject to an extensive restoration, with the original colour scheme reinstated in the library. These works have caused some contention as the new colour scheme does not adhere to Adam's drawings. However, it is important to remember that drawings were mere suggestions from an architect to his client and it cannot be assumed that they perfectly represent what was actually built.

Robert Adam, elevation of the Royal Terrace at the Adelphi, London, advertisement drawing, 1769–72, SM Adam volume 32/10. Photograph: Geremy Butler.

From 1768 the Adam brothers pooled their efforts in order to undertake a speculative development of London townhouses on the northern bank of the River Thames known as the Adelphi: Greek for 'brothers'. Being vast in scale, and supported by vaulted undercrofts, the scheme brought the Adam family close to financial ruin. This drawing offers a fine elevation of the Royal Terrace, the most prominent street within the complex, overlooking the river. The first resident of the Adelphi was the Shakespearean actor David Garrick, who took a 96-year lease of number 5 Royal Terrace, the central house in the block. Garrick agreed that the Adam brothers could use his name as an inducement to other potential residents in an advertisement for *Town and Country Magazine*, and this drawing is part of a series made of the Royal Terrace and Garrick's individual house at number 5. It is interesting to note that the exact pattern of windows and doors is not shown here as built. The entrance to Garrick's three-bay house was not perfectly central, but rather, in reality, was moved to the left-hand side in order to maximize interior space. Clearly a degree of artistic licence has been used here in order to make the Adelphi appear even more glamorous than it already was. In 1775 Robert and James Adam became Garrick's neighbours when they moved into number 4 Royal Terrace. Nothing remains of these houses, however, as the central block of the development was demolished in 1936.

→• Attributed to William Hamilton or Joseph Bonomi for Robert and James Adam, plan of the glass drawing room ceiling, Northumberland House, Strand, London, 1770, SM Adam volume 11/33. Photograph: Geremy Butler.

Northumberland House was the London home of the 1st Duke and Duchess of Northumberland. It was a fine Jacobean townhouse for which the wealthy Duke and Duchess commissioned improvements, including a drawing room by Adam. The room is famous for having had walls lined with painted glass and gilt metalwork, but the ceiling was no less awe-inspiring, being densely polychromed and ornamented with plasterwork and inset painted panels. There was a central painted medallion enclosed within an octagon with four radiating arms connecting to painted lunettes. Being designed for such a learned pair as the Duke and Duchess of Northumberland, the ceiling was inspired by that in the da Udine-Peruzzi loggia at the Villa Madama in Rome. This is Adam's most colourful surviving presentation drawing and offers a mere glimpse of this singular composition. The ceiling was destroyed with the demolition of the house in 1874 in order to make way for Northumberland Avenue, and this drawing is the best surviving record of its appearance.

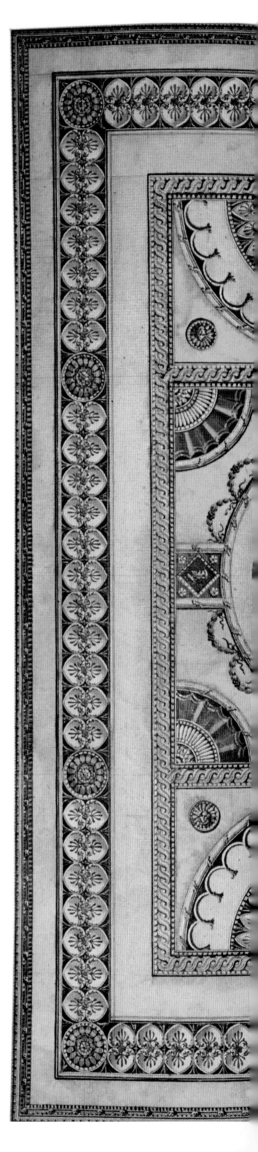

Michael Rysbrack fecit.

●— **John Michael Rysbrack, elevation of a funerary monument to Sir Nathaniel Curzon at the church of All Saints, Kedleston, Derbyshire, to a design by Robert Adam, 1765, SM volume 37/8. Photograph: Ardon Bar-Hama.**

The Flemish sculptor John Michael (Johannes Michel) Rysbrack spent the majority of his career in England, arriving in 1720 and quickly establishing himself as one of the pre-eminent sculptors in the country: a position he maintained until his death. He was particularly noted for his portrait sculpture and, as such, became popular as a sculptor of funerary monuments. This drawing depicts a monument to Sir Nathaniel Curzon, 4th Baronet of Kedleston Hall in Derbyshire, whose eldest son, also Sir Nathaniel, commissioned Robert Adam in *c.*1759 to design this monument for the north transept of the church of All Saints, which is immediately adjacent to Kedleston Hall. Rysbrack sculpted the monument in accordance with Adam's design, signing his work in 1763, and it is likely that he made this drawing two years later as a record of his work. It is now contained in a volume of drawings by significant sculptors including Rysbrack himself, Peter Scheemakers (1691–1781) and Joseph Nollekens, which was purchased by Soane in July 1823 from a sale of the possessions of the latter.

Attributed to Joseph Bonomi for Robert Adam, profile elevation of a funerary monument to Lady Caroline Milton at Milton Abbey, Dorset, 1775, SM Adam volume 19/63. Photograph: Ardon Bar-Hama.

Robert Adam's monument to Lady Caroline Milton was commissioned by her husband, Baron Milton, whose grief is known to have been considerable: three years after her death Horace Walpole reported that Milton had been reclusive ever since. The monument survives *in situ* and comprises a Gothic or castle-style couch, carved by Agostino Carlini RA. The couch adheres exactly to Adam's design and is surmounted by two reclining figures in medieval dress, that of Lady Caroline sleeping, with Milton propped up on his elbow to gaze upon his wife. For its date of 1775, the design is an oddity and it is Adam's only funerary monument to deviate from his typical Neo-classical style. The elegance of the design shown in this drawing is clear, but the reason for its style is less so. It may have been associated with the context of Milton Abbey itself, or by the context of Lord Milton's rebuilding work of 1771–6 at Milton Abbey House to designs by Sir William Chambers, where a surviving medieval hall had been incorporated. Either way, Adam's innovative foray into the neo-Gothic appears to be an exciting precursor to monuments of the Victorian period.

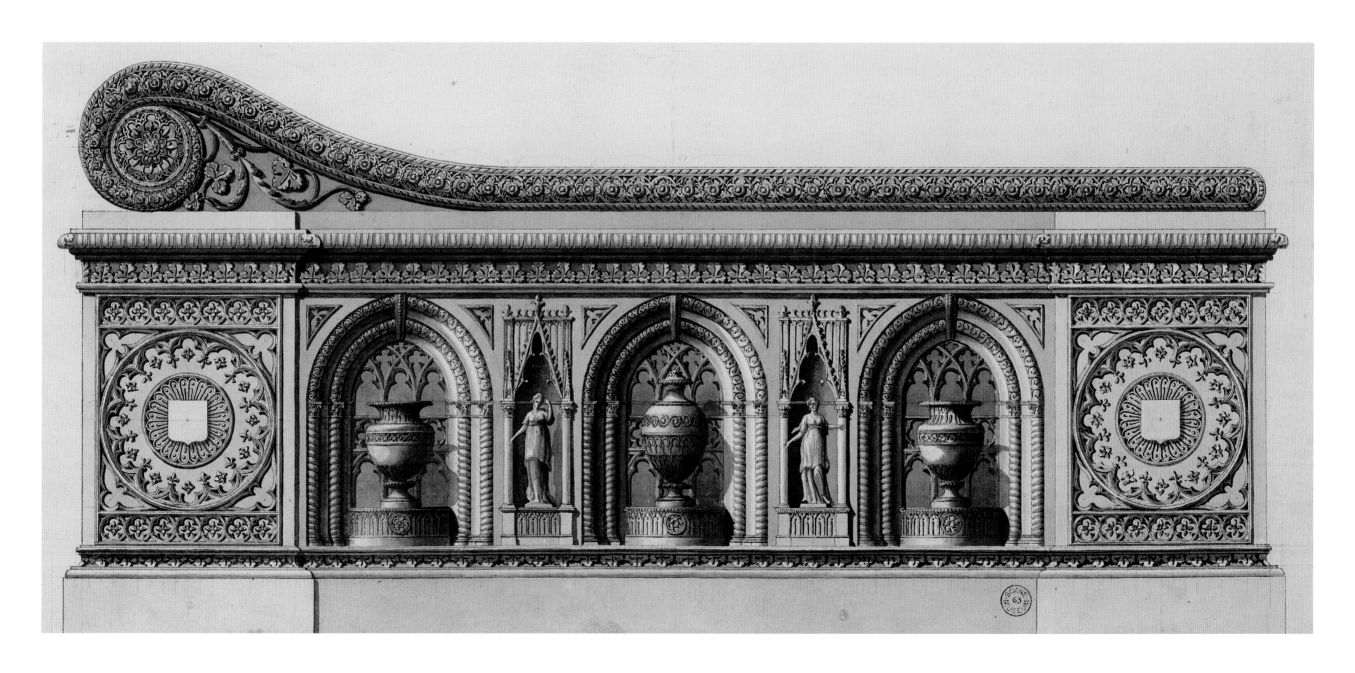

➔• Attributed to Joseph Bonomi for Robert and James Adam, elevation of the state bed at Osterley Park, Isleworth, 1776, SM Adam volume 17/157. Photograph: Ardon Bar-Hama.

Originally an Elizabethan quadrangular house, Osterley was much altered throughout the late seventeenth and eighteenth centuries, largely by the Child banking dynasty. The Child family had taken possession of Osterley in 1713 after the previous owner, Dr Nicholas Barbon, had defaulted on a mortgage from the Child Bank. In the 1760s and 1770s, work on the house included Adam's interior decoration of the principal rooms, including the state apartment of tapestry room, state bedchamber and Etruscan dressing room in the south range of the house. It is widely known that Adam's wealthier clients were able to commission designs for everything from the architecture of their house down to their silverware, and this design for the Osterley state bed is a magnificent example of Adam's skill as a furniture designer. Executed by the cabinetmaker John Linnell, and surviving *in situ* with its original green hangings, it is a four-poster, domed canopy bed with paired fluted posts. Adam's inspiration for this state bed has been variously suggested as the Choragic Monument of Lysicrates at Athens and the Temple of Venus at Pomona.

—•Attributed to Joseph Bonomi for Robert and James Adam, sections of the stairwell at Home House, 20 Portman Square, London, *c.*1777, SM Adam volume 14/116. Photograph: Ardon Bar-Hama.

Elizabeth, Countess of Home, was the twice-widowed daughter of a Jamaican plantation owner and was an inordinately wealthy lady. Moreover, she was strong-minded and unusual. William Beckford reported that the 'riff raff' referred to her as the 'Queen of Hell' on account of her notoriously irascible behaviour and lavish parties. In 1772, aged 68, she began to build a magnificent new townhouse at 20 Portman Square to designs by James Wyatt (1746–1813), but Wyatt's slow pace of work frustrated the Countess, and in 1775 he was replaced by Adam. Adam's principal responsibilities at Home House were for the interior decoration, but he also made some structural alterations, forming a circuit of social spaces, including his most successful urban stairwell. This presentation drawing for the stairwell offers a double section, as if the space has been sliced in two, and opened like a dolls' house. It shows the stairwell as executed, being a top-lit oval space with an imposing Imperial staircase (with flights divided from a half landing) and dense plasterwork ornamentation to the walls.

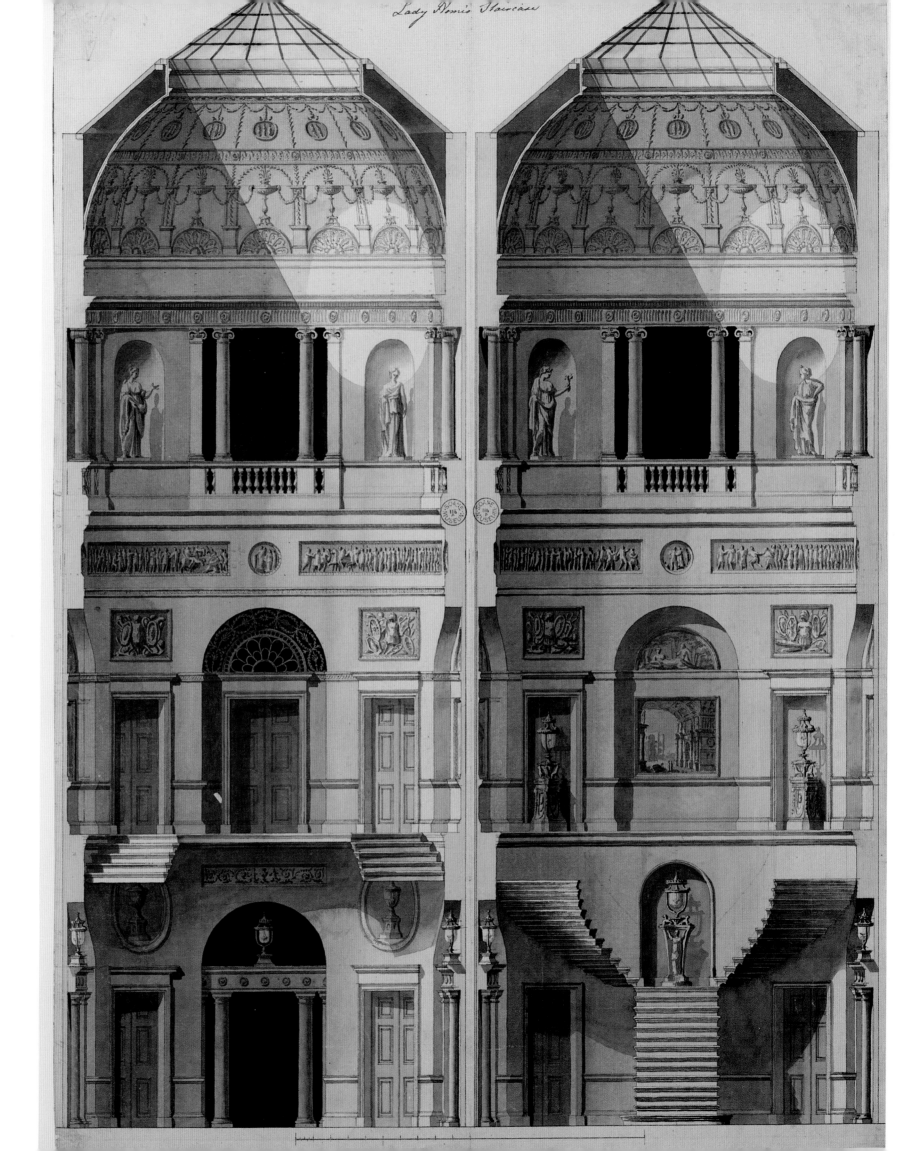

● Attributed to Robert Morison for Robert and James Adam, elevation of the window wall for the drawing room at Cumberland House, Pall Mall, London, 1780–5, SM Adam volume 49/19. Photograph: Ardon Bar-Hama.

This drawing illustrates one of the most alluring interior schemes in Adam's mature style, with grotesque panels intended to be executed in shallow relief, and an unusual amount of gilding. It was designed for one of three drawing rooms at Cumberland House, which from 1772 was the home of Prince Henry Frederick, Duke of Cumberland and Strathearn, a naval officer and the youngest brother of King George III. Having been exiled from court by his brother on account of an unsuitable marriage to a commoner

(prompting the Royal Marriages Act in 1772), Cumberland suffered considerable financial difficulties and spent much of his time on the Continent. When in London, however, he continually sought to improve Cumberland House to Adam's designs, commissioning schemes for the music room, great dining room, private eating room, boudoir, three breathtaking drawing rooms and an entirely new wing for the Duchess's notoriously vulgar sister. It has been suggested that these proposed enhancements were intended to produce a social alternative to the royal court, in which the Cumberlands could entertain their own social circle. Unfortunately, these fine interiors remained largely unrealized as Cumberland simply could not afford to undertake the necessary works.

JOHN SOANE AND THE SOANE OFFICE DRAWINGS

There are around 8,000 drawings within the Soane office drawings collection, including Soane's Grand Tour drawings, his office drawings, exhibition drawings and Royal Academy lecture drawings (see page 16). These have been preserved at the Soane Museum since Soane's death in 1837.

Soane on the Grand Tour

—• **John Soane, plan and elevation of the Temple of Neptune, Paestum, being a page from a sketchbook made during his Grand Tour, 1779, SM volume 39/15 verso-16 recto. Photograph: Hugh Kelly.**

Having received the King's travelling studentship, Soane was able to undertake an educational Grand Tour from 1778 (see page 8). Many of his observational Grand Tour drawings were lost as he travelled home in 1780, but the volume in which these drawings are found has survived. It is small, bound in waterproof vellum with a flap and vellum tie, clearly being intended for travel and to be held with one hand, perhaps while standing, and leaving the other hand free to write or draw. It is a volume of the type made in Italy and was certainly purchased by Soane as a sketchbook prior to a journey he made between 4 January and 24 March 1779, when he left Rome in order to visit – among other places – Pozzuoli, Pompeii, Paestum, Salerno, Naples, Capua and Albano, all of which are represented in the volume. The last entry was made on 24 March on the Appian Way on Soane's return to Rome. This particular opening in the volume was made on 26 or 27 January 1779 when Soane visited the ruined Greek colonial city of Paestum to the south of Naples, and here we can see a plan and elevation of the principal temple there, the Temple of Neptune. Although these sketches are rough and obviously made *en plein air*, Soane certainly intended to use them as a pattern book for future reference as we can see from details such as his note: '20 flutes to each Column'. The detail of a moulding adjacent to the elevation suggests that Soane had bravely climbed up the columns in order to make a close examination. Although the Temple of Neptune was influential over Soane's later work, it cannot be assumed that his admiration of it was entirely unadulterated. On a return visit to Paestum a month later he wrote in the same volume that he found the 'Architecture of the three Temples [at Paestum] ... exceedingly rude ... all the parts of the Grecian doric but not the elegance & taste'.

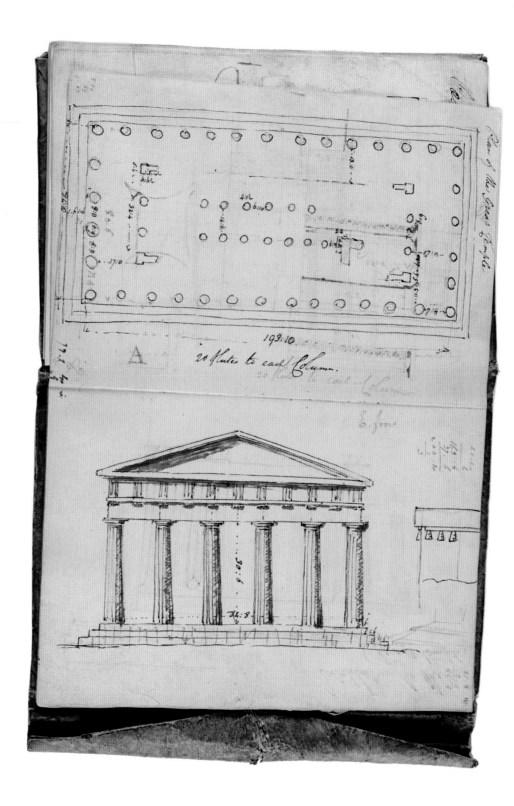

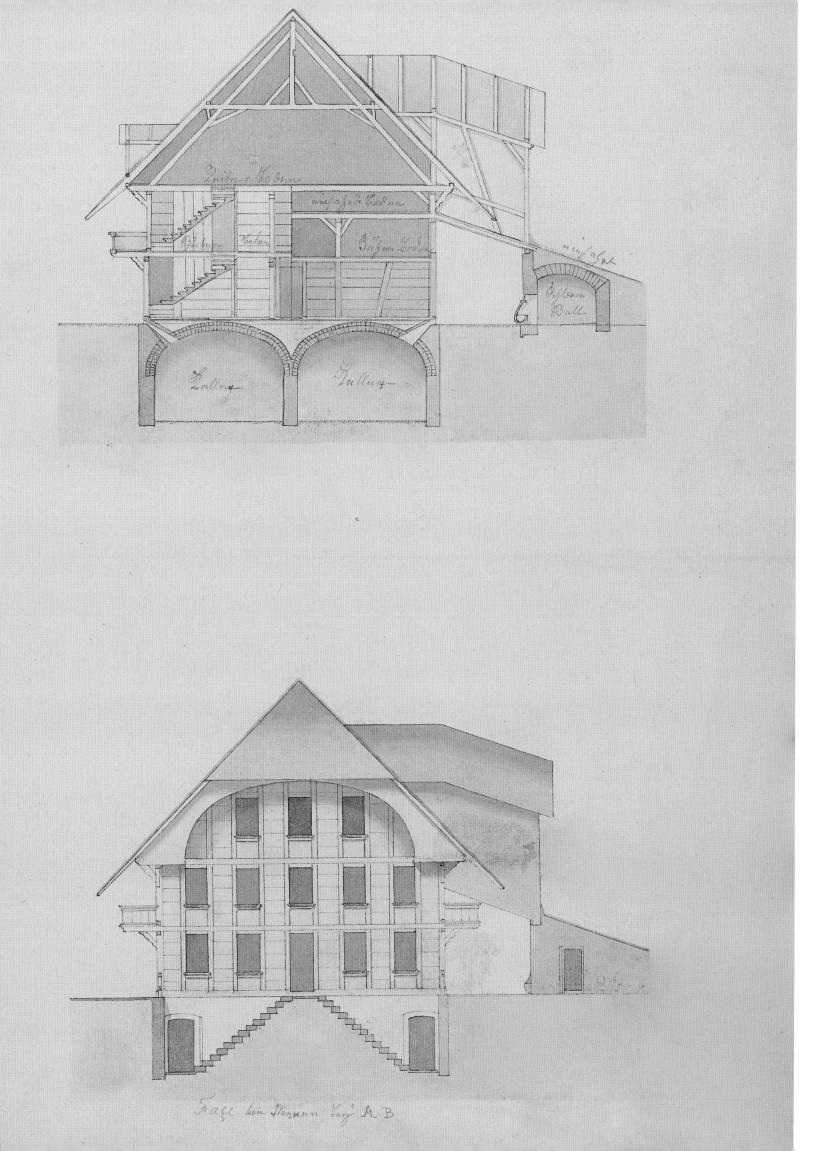

— **Thomas Sword for Sir John Soane**, copy of a Swiss drawing showing an elevation and section of a Swiss farmhouse, Surso, 20 September 1800, SM 48/4/13. Photograph: Ardon Bar-Hama. This drawing is something of a rarity in Soane's collection as it is a mystery. Soane had travelled through Switzerland as he returned home from his Grand Tour in 1780, and during that time he particularly admired the Swiss wooden bridges and the farmhouses. However, this drawing illustrating a Swiss farmhouse at an unknown place called Surso (possibly Sursee in Lucerne) is in the hand of Thomas Sword (ND), a Soane office pupil, and was made on 20 September 1800, long after Soane had visited Switzerland. The draughtsman has clearly taken great care over this drawing, producing an elevation and section of a timber-framed house, supported by brick-built vaulted cellars and surmounted by a steeply pitched roof as is appropriate in regions with heavy snowfall. For what purpose the drawing was made is entirely obscure and moreover, so is the source of the design. Certainly, Soane maintained his interest in Switzerland long after his Grand Tour as he purchased two editions of William Coxe's *Travels in Switzerland* (1789 and 1801). However, there are no plates within this publication that illustrate farmhouses nor is 'Surso' mentioned.

↓ **Joseph Michael Gandy for Sir John Soane**, RA lecture drawing, bird's-eye view of a penitentiary house for 600 male convicts, originally designed by Soane in 1781 as part of a competition, 2 July 1799, SM 13/1/19. Photograph: Geremy Butler.

Soane office drawings

●— Office of Sir John Soane, view of the interior of the Rotunda at the Bank of England, London, 1798, SM 9/2/1C. Photograph: Geremy Butler.

The Bank of England was the major commission of Soane's architectural career, lasting 45 years from 1788 until 1833, and was referred to by Soane himself as 'the pride and boast of my life'. He admired the elegance and durability of Roman domes, such as that of the Pantheon in Rome, and used domes throughout his career, including this example in the Bank's Rotunda, a space for trading government and Bank stocks. Here, Soane shows the interior completely empty, devoid of desks or banking paraphernalia, enabling the viewer to focus solely on the beauty of his architecture and to more easily draw a comparison with the Pantheon.

—● Joseph Michael Gandy for Sir John Soane, imaginary view of the Rotunda and the Dividend Warrant Office at the Bank of England in ruins, 1798, SM P127. Photograph: Geremy Butler.

Soane's Rotunda at the Bank of England was completed in 1798, the same year that Gandy created this drawing showing it as a ruin. Presenting the space in decay may seem a rather odd means of celebrating its construction, but we must consider Soane's fascination with ruins, and his certainty that like the ruins of antique Rome, it would be valued even into dilapidation. The drawing was exhibited at the RA in 1832, a whole 34 years after its creation, and as Soane was retiring as Architect to the Bank. That Soane should delve into the past and select this particular drawing to mark his departure from the Bank would suggest that the Rotunda was his most treasured achievement within the entire complex. At the RA, the drawing was given the title *Architectural Ruins – A Vision*, and was aptly accompanied by Shakespeare's lines from *The Tempest*:

> *The cloud-capt towers, the gorgeous palaces,*
> *the solemn temples, the great globe itself,*
> *Yea, all which it inherit shall dissolve.*

●— **Joseph Michael Gandy for Sir John Soane, view of Tyringham church by moonlight, 1798, SM P269. Photograph: Hugh Kelly.**
The house and park buildings at Tyringham comprised Soane's largest country house project. It was commissioned by a banker, William Praed, with whom Soane had become acquainted through his work at the Bank of England. The house itself he designed *in toto* from 1797, and it was one of Soane's happiest projects, doubtless as he was given considerable free rein over the design. Upon completion of the project, Gandy spent nine days there from 27 July to 7 August 1798 in order to make a series of exquisite presentation and exhibition drawings for Soane to record and commemorate his work. This drawing of Soane's unexecuted design for the church was not made during Gandy's visit, but is roughly contemporary and was included among Soane's exhibition drawings of Tyringham. It is incredibly dramatic, being depicted at night by the light of a full moon, and with lamplight shining from the interior of the building. What prompted Gandy to illustrate the unexecuted church design at night is not known, but Soane was certainly pleased with the result as he chose to display it in the North Drawing Room at 13 Lincoln's Inn Fields.

→● Joseph Michael Gandy and Antonio Van Assen for Sir John Soane, view of the principal façade of Pitzhanger Manor, Ealing, 1800, SM 14/2/3. Photograph: Geremy Butler.

Pitzhanger is a suburban villa one hour by carriage from Lincoln's Inn Fields, although Soane is known to have frequently made the journey on foot. He had bought the house on 5 September 1800 for £4,500, before largely rebuilding it between 1800 and 1804, and then using it for social gatherings and entertaining friends. In this exhibition drawing, the proposed design for Soane's new central block takes prominence, with an entrance front that is reminiscent of the Arch of Constantine in Rome, thereby offering a subtle connection between Soane's own work and that of the admired antique building. However, we can also glimpse a secondary, pre-existing wing, cast in shadow on the left-hand side. Soane had worked on the left-hand wing – an extension to the original house

– as an apprentice to George Dance when Soane was only 15 years old, and it is a testament to his experience at that time, as well as his regard for Dance, that the wing was retained. The family in the foreground of the drawing are a clue as to Soane's intentions for the house. He hoped that the project would inspire his two sons to take up the architectural profession and that they might inherit the house as a Soane family seat. This was not to be the case (see page 8) and by 1809 Soane's architectural practice was so busy that he had little time to spend in Ealing. As a result, he sold Pitzhanger in 1810, and instead focused his efforts on the house and collection at Lincoln's Inn Fields. This drawing was made in the year that Soane purchased Pitzhanger, and may have been the design for his proposed works there, which was included in the RA exhibition of 1801, perhaps as an advertisement of Soane's abilities given the freedom of being his own client. Indeed, he described Pitzhanger as a self-portrait.

●— **Joseph Michael Gandy for Sir John Soane, view of the Scala Regia at the House of Lords, Palace of Westminster, London, 19 August 1800, SM P283. Photograph: Hugh Kelly.**

In 1814, Soane was appointed as Attached Architect to the Office of Works, with responsibility for the areas of Whitehall and Westminster. Over the following 17 years he undertook a number of projects in this capacity, and from 1822 these included a prominent new entrance to the Palace of Westminster for the King's processional route from Old Palace Yard to the House of Lords. The grand Scala Regia (Royal Stair) was built in 1822–3 and gave access to a magnificent new Royal Gallery. As we can see in this drawing by Gandy, every element of the design was monumental, from the coffered barrel vault or the vast semi-circular clerestory window, to the sculpted figures of past monarchs, which were doubtless intended to gain the approbation of King George III.

──● **Office of Sir John Soane, elevation of the capital from the Temple of Vesta, Tivoli, *c.*1810–36, SM volume 83/53. Photograph: Ardon Bar-Hama.**

From September 1784 Soane began to accept articled pupils whom he instructed in the Art, Profession and Business of architecture (see page 16). The first task for any student would have been to learn to draw, and this was achieved through the actions of observation and rendition of objects from Soane's collection. This drawing is extremely accomplished, and it is a shame that we do not know which of Soane's pupils was responsible for it. It illustrates the Corinthian capital from Soane's favourite building: the Temple of Vesta at Tivoli. The exact source for this drawing from among Soane's collection is unknown, but there are various options including Soane's own Grand Tour sketchbook (SM volume 40/71 verso), or a book in Soane's library such as Antoine Desgodetz's *Les édifices antiques de Rome ...* (1682), which was purchased at an unknown date, but was included in Soane's portrait by William Owen in 1804 (SM P228) open at the very page showing the Temple of Vesta at Tivoli.

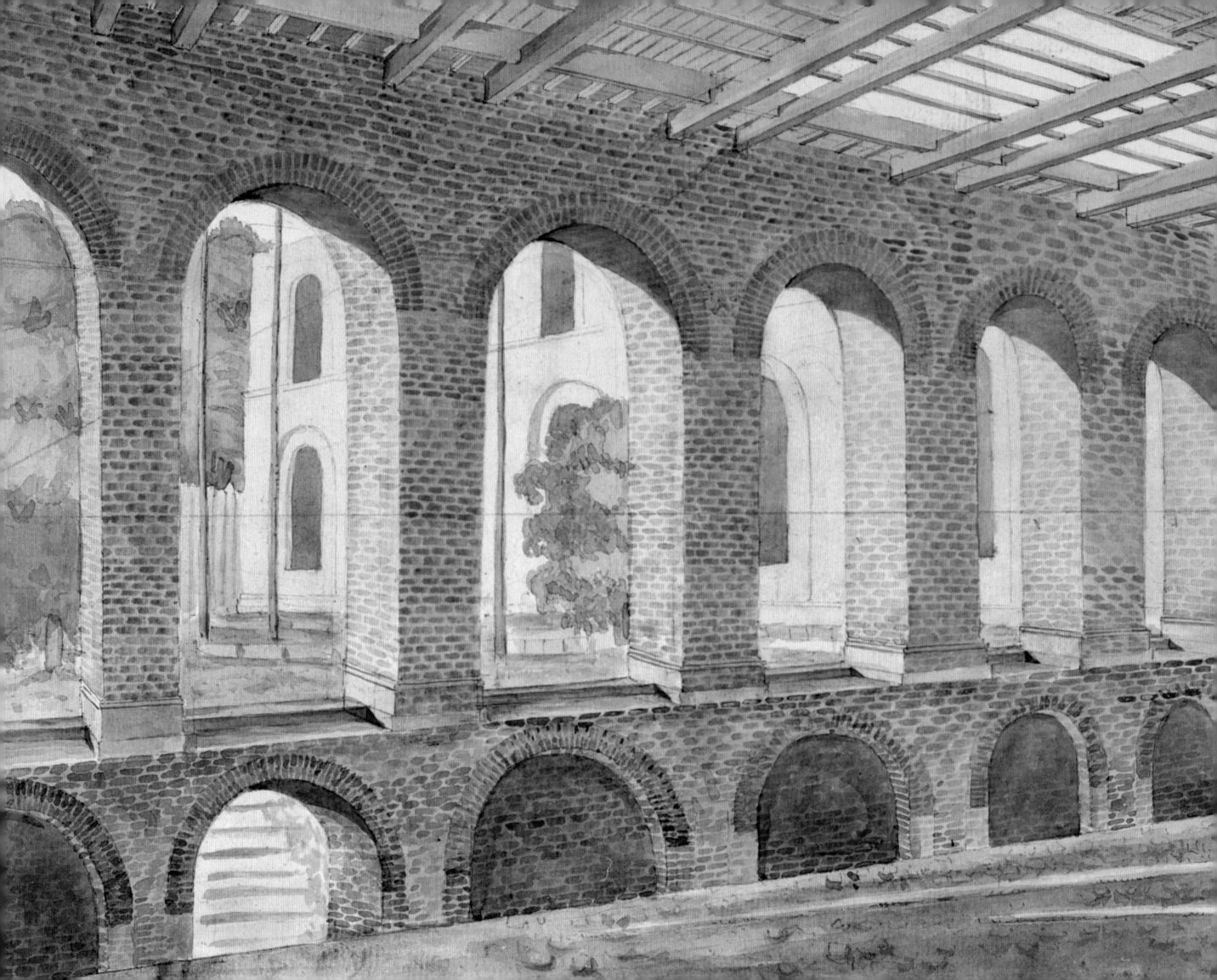

•— Office of Sir John Soane, view of the interior of the arcade at the New Infirmary for the Royal Hospital, Chelsea, progress drawing, 1810, SM volume 76/24. Photograph: Geremy Butler. Soane's apprentices usually spent their time making drawings or running errands, but from 1810 onwards they would also be fortunate enough to visit a selection of Soane's building sites across London in order to observe and sketch the progress of construction. This was not a means of updating their master, but was intended to familiarize the students with building processes and was another part of their training. This example of a progress drawing illustrates part of the New Infirmary at the Royal Hospital, Chelsea, which was built from 1810. It is most interesting to see here the courses of brick, the brick arcading and the timber joists – the internal skeleton of the building – without their coating of plaster. Soane had been Clerk of Works to the Royal Hospital since 1807, and this site, along with the Bank of England, offered excellent opportunities for his students to undertake this type of observational work. Soane maintained his role at Chelsea until his death, and prized it highly, not least because it afforded him the Clerk of Works' house there, which increasingly became his country retreat, especially after the sale of Pitzhanger Manor in 1810.

—• Office of Sir John Soane, view of the interior of the mausoleum at Dulwich Picture Gallery with a Soane office pupil drawing, progress drawing, August 1812, SM volume 81/23. Photograph: Geremy Butler.

●— George Basevi for Sir John Soane, elevation of a cast of the entablature of the Temple of Castor and Pollux, Rome, 1812, SM volume 53/15. Photograph: Ardon Bar-Hama.

This accomplished pencil drawing depicts a cast of the entablature of the Temple of Castor and Pollux in Rome. It was a building Soane admired greatly, and so in 1801, he acquired full-sized casts of its capital and entablature (SM M47 and SM M45) for his collection and the benefit of his office. The drawing is from a volume of drawings by Soane's apprentice George Basevi (1794–1845), made in 1812, and containing sketches of various objects within Soane's collection. It is evident that Basevi was an extremely talented young man. He was one of Soane's pupils in 1811–16, winning the admiration of his master, and then went on to become an architect in his own right. Basevi was probably the most successful of all Soane's former apprentices, but did not equal Soane's prolific output, as he died tragically, aged only 50. While inspecting the belfry at Ely Cathedral he fell through the floorboards to the floor below.

➤ George Basevi for Sir John Soane, view of the Soane Monument, St Giles-in-the-Fields burial ground, St Pancras, London, set within an imaginary landscape, 1816, SM 14/4/9. Photograph: Hugh Kelly.

Just seven weeks after his wife, Eliza's death on 22 November 1815, Soane set about making designs for a family funerary monument. This view depicts the monument as executed, but within an exquisite fantasy landscape, rather than the confines of St Giles-in-the-Fields burial ground. The drawing is in the hand of George Basevi, whose loyalty to his master was demonstrated by his remaining in the Soane office several months beyond the expiry of his apprentice's articles, even refusing £25 in pay from Soane, in order to continue his work on the Soane Monument. The west side of the monument carries Eliza's epitaph, written by the Soanes' close friend, Mrs Barbara Hofland. On Soane's own death in 1837, he was interred in the monument alongside his wife and their eldest son, John, who had died of tuberculosis in 1823.

●— **Office of Sir John Soane, view of the west front of Dulwich Picture Gallery under construction, progress drawing, 1812, SM 65/4/47. Photograph: Geremy Butler.**

This progress drawing gives a view of Dulwich Picture Gallery under construction, drawn at some time during the summer of 1812, and includes some fascinating details, such as the scaffolding, wooden arch proformas and the carcass of the famous mausoleum. The gallery was built to house a collection of paintings that had belonged to Noel Desenfans (1744–1807) and Sir Peter Francis Bougeois RA (1753–1811). Following their deaths, Dulwich College received both the collection and the sum of £3,000 in order to assist in refurbishing or rebuilding their gallery, as well as building a mausoleum to the benefactors. Desenfans and Bourgeois had been Soane's friends and former patrons, and so Soane took the commission to build a new gallery for the college without a fee, and worked on the project from 1811–13. Soane was clearly pleased with this drawing as an enlarged version was produced as an RA lecture drawing in 1815 (SM 15/2/11), although in this the draughtsman has also included trees and workmen in order to offer a sense of scale.

Office of Sir John Soane, bird's-eye view of the Bank of England as it was 1810, 9 July 1810, SM 1/8/12. Photograph: Hugh Kelly.

→ Office of Sir John Soane, view of the interior of the South-east Transfer Office at the Bank of England, London, 1820–1, SM 11/4/2. Photograph: Geremy Butler.

Soane's work at the Bank of England spanned the years 1788-1833 and comprised a number of different building campaigns. The South-east Transfer Office was built in 1817–23 to the south-east of Soane's Rotunda. Like the Rotunda, this space illustrates perfectly the way in which the offices and banking halls were densely packed into a single 'city block', and so it was necessary for Soane to fenestrate and light the spaces from above. This presentation drawing offers a calm and business-like view of the interior of the South-east Transfer Office, proffering Soane's interior decorative design to the Bank Commissioners for approval at around the time that the mighty fabric of the space was nearing completion. Soane's elegant and attenuated mouldings are seen here to best effect, largely thanks to the cool colour scheme of the Bank interior and the skilful depiction of sunlight streaming through the central lantern. Staffage is added in order to offer some perception of scale and thereby increase the viewer's sensation of awe at Soane's architecture.

● Joseph Michael Gandy for Sir John Soane, bird's-eye, cutaway view of the Bank of England as completed, 1830, SM P267. Photograph: Geremy Butler.

This slightly overwhelming drawing represents the vast accumulated works undertaken by Soane at the Bank of England, as complete in 1830, offering an impressive level of intricacy, which had been achieved over his numerous building campaigns. The drawing is often referred to as 'the Bank in ruins', suggesting a mythical future in which the much-admired building had been preserved even in its state of decay. Certainly the ground beside the building is collapsing away, but the building is actually a cutaway, offering a clever combination of plan, elevation and section in order to display the interior of the complex. It was exhibited at the RA in 1830 as a celebration, and perhaps even a boast, of Soane's achievements at the Bank. It was accompanied by a quotation from Alain René Le Sage's popular novel *Gil Blas*: '*Je vais enlever les toits de cette superbe édifice national … le dedans va se découvrir à vos yeux de même qu'on voit le dedans un pâté don't on vient d'ôter la croûte* [I want to lift the roof of that wonderful national building … The interior will be revealed to you like a meat pie with the crust removed]'. Since its return from the RA in 1830, the drawing has hung inside the movable planes in the North Drawing Room at 13 Lincoln's Inn Fields, suggesting its significance in that Soane had always intended it to be exhibited within his museum.

RA lecture drawings

⎮ Office of Sir John Soane, RA lecture drawing, perspective view of Thomas Sandby's design for a Bridge of Magnificence over the River Thames, 1806–19, SM 21/1/11. Photograph: Geremy Butler.

━● Office of Sir John Soane, RA lecture drawing, cutaway section through the Temple of Neptune, Paestum, 9 August 1806, SM 19/5/3. Photograph: Ardon Bar-Hama.

This lecture drawing illustrates the Temple of Neptune at Paestum in Italy, which Soane had seen during his Grand Tour in 1779. In the hand of an unknown draughtsman from Soane's office, the drawing is a copy from an engraving in Giovanni Battista Piranesi's *Différentes vues de Pesto ...* of 1778. Soane later acquired 15 of Piranesi's preparatory Paestum drawings in 1817. (See page 135.)

●— Giovanni Battista Piranesi, view of the Temple of Neptune, Paestum, drawing made for publication, 1777–8, SM P72. Photograph: The National Gallery, London.

On the advice of Sir William Chambers, when he arrived in Rome at the start of his Grand Tour in November 1778, the young Soane sought out Giovanni Battista Piranesi, a Venetian designer and renowned draughtsman. Just months before Piranesi's death, this meeting, and Piranesi's work generally, would have a profound and lasting influence over Soane's architectural style and handling of space, just as it had over other British architects including Robert Adam and George Dance the Younger. Soane collected Piranesi's published engravings and original drawings whenever possible. In 1777, Piranesi had made a detailed study of Paestum, an abandoned and ruined Greek colonial city south of Naples, where he produced

a series of drawings in preparation for the publication of *Différentes vues de Pesto* … which appeared posthumously in 1778, having been completed by Piranesi's son Francesco. Of the 17 surviving preparatory drawings made for the plates, 15 were purchased by Soane in 1817 and this example shows the Temple of Neptune from the north-east, with the Basilica on the left-hand side. Like its siblings, this drawing's vividly sketch-like surface conveys the play of light and dramatic appearance of the ruins, which is further emphasized by Piranesi's artistic licence, including the addition of appropriately rustic staffage and the use of multiple vanishing points. Piranesi never made finished drawings in preparation for his etchings as he felt that this would detract from the spontaneous expression within the act of engraving.

Giovanni Battista Piranesi, view of the interior of the Temple of Neptune, Paestum, from within the peristyle at the west end, looking south, drawing made for publication, 1777–8, SM P74. Photograph: The National Gallery, London.

● ─ Henry Parke for Sir John Soane, RA lecture drawing, view of a student on a ladder, with a rod measuring the Corinthian order of the Temple of Castor and Pollux, Rome, 1806–19, SM 23/9/3. Photograph: Ardon Bar-Hama.

In the hand of Soane's apprentice Henry Parke (1790–1835), this drawing illustrates the precarious activity of scaling buildings in order to better observe their ornamental details in the upper register. This is something that many Grand Tourists did and something that we know Soane himself had done during his Grand Tour. In his second lecture Soane discussed the Corinthian order, claiming that *'the most sublime and awefully grand and impressive'* example was to be found on the Temple of Castor and Pollux in the Forum at Rome – the very building seen in this drawing – and he described the capital as *'full of originality and peculiar grace; the effect of the caulicoli, entwined in each other, is uncommonly beautiful, and highly rational, the abacus cannot be sufficiently admired'*. (Sir John Soane, RA lecture 2.) Soane so admired the Corinthian capital of the Temple of Castor and Pollux that in 1801 he acquired a full-sized cast of it, as well as one of the entablature (SM M47 and SM M45), placing them in his museum to allow close observation.

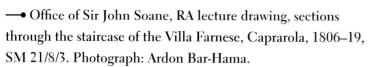 **Office of Sir John Soane, RA lecture drawing, sections through the staircase of the Villa Farnese, Caprarola, 1806–19, SM 21/8/3. Photograph: Ardon Bar-Hama.**

The Villa Farnese was built as a fortified castle from 1504 but was then converted into a pleasure villa in 1559 for Cardinal Alessandro Farnese to designs by Giacomo Barozzi da Vignola (1507–73). This drawing in an unknown Soane office hand shows two sections of Vignola's extraordinary spiral staircase at the Villa Farnese, offering a sensational vantage point, which of course would not have been possible in reality without demolishing the building. Soane used the drawing in his fifth lecture to praise Vignola's careful observance of Vitruvius and stated that his buildings – including the Villa Farnese – *'can never be sufficiently admired or too much studied'*.

→ Office of Sir John Soane, RA lecture drawing, comparative elevations of St Peter's, Rome and St Paul's Cathedral, London, 1806–19, SM 75/1/7. Photograph: Ardon Bar-Hama.

● — Charles Tyrrell for Sir John Soane, RA lecture drawing, comparative elevations and sections of St Peter's and the Pantheon, Rome, the Radcliffe Library, Oxford and the Rotunda at the Bank of England, London, 1806–19, SM 23/2/2. Photograph: Geremy Butler.

This drawing by Soane's apprentice Charles Tyrrell (1795–1832) is among a group of ten lecture drawings of ancient and modern buildings juxtaposed with one another to illustrate their respective scales. This particular example compares the proportions of four of the most significant domed buildings in England and Italy. In the background St Peter's looms over its siblings like a much admired but shadowy ancestor; with the three smaller buildings in the foreground – the Pantheon, the Radcliffe Library and the Rotunda at the Bank of England – illuminated as if to express their comparative accessibility as feats of architecture and construction. It is rather clever that the Pantheon and Rotunda are both shown in section as Soane is making a clear analogy between the Pantheon's famed structural ingenuity and his own masterpiece at the Bank of England. Soane used this drawing as a climactic last illustration in his twelfth and final lecture. He was pleased to compare his own dome over the Rotunda with Michelangelo's dome at St Peter's, as they were both constructed of incombustible materials, unlike Wren's vulnerable timber dome and the vaulted ceiling at St Paul's Cathedral, which is compared rather unfavourably with the magnificence of St Peter's in the previous drawing.

➤ **George Bailey for Sir John Soane, RA lecture drawing, comparative elevation and section of the Colosseum, Rome and the Circus, Bath, 1806–19, SM 23/2/1. Photograph: Geremy Butler.**

Like the previous drawing, which compares the scales of four domed buildings, this drawing by Soane's apprentice George Bailey is part of the same group, and rather comically juxtaposes two similarly ornamented segmental façades: one half of the mighty Colosseum in Rome and John Wood's comparably squat Circus in Bath. Soane used this drawing during his tenth lecture when discussing the successful and unsuccessful ways in which architects throughout history had used tiers of classical columns – or orders – as embellishments to the exterior of buildings. He complained that the orders on Wood's Circus were too short: 'The Circus at Bath, may please us by its prettiness and a sort of novelty, as a rattle pleases a child, but the area is so small, and the height of each of the orders is so diminutive, that the general appearance of the entire building is mean, gloomy, and confined, and very inferior in effect to the crescent in the same city. What is justly admired on the large scale of the Colosseum, becomes uninteresting, nay even ridiculous, when reduced to the dimensions and extent necessary for a few modern dwelling houses.' (Sir John Soane, RA lecture 10.)

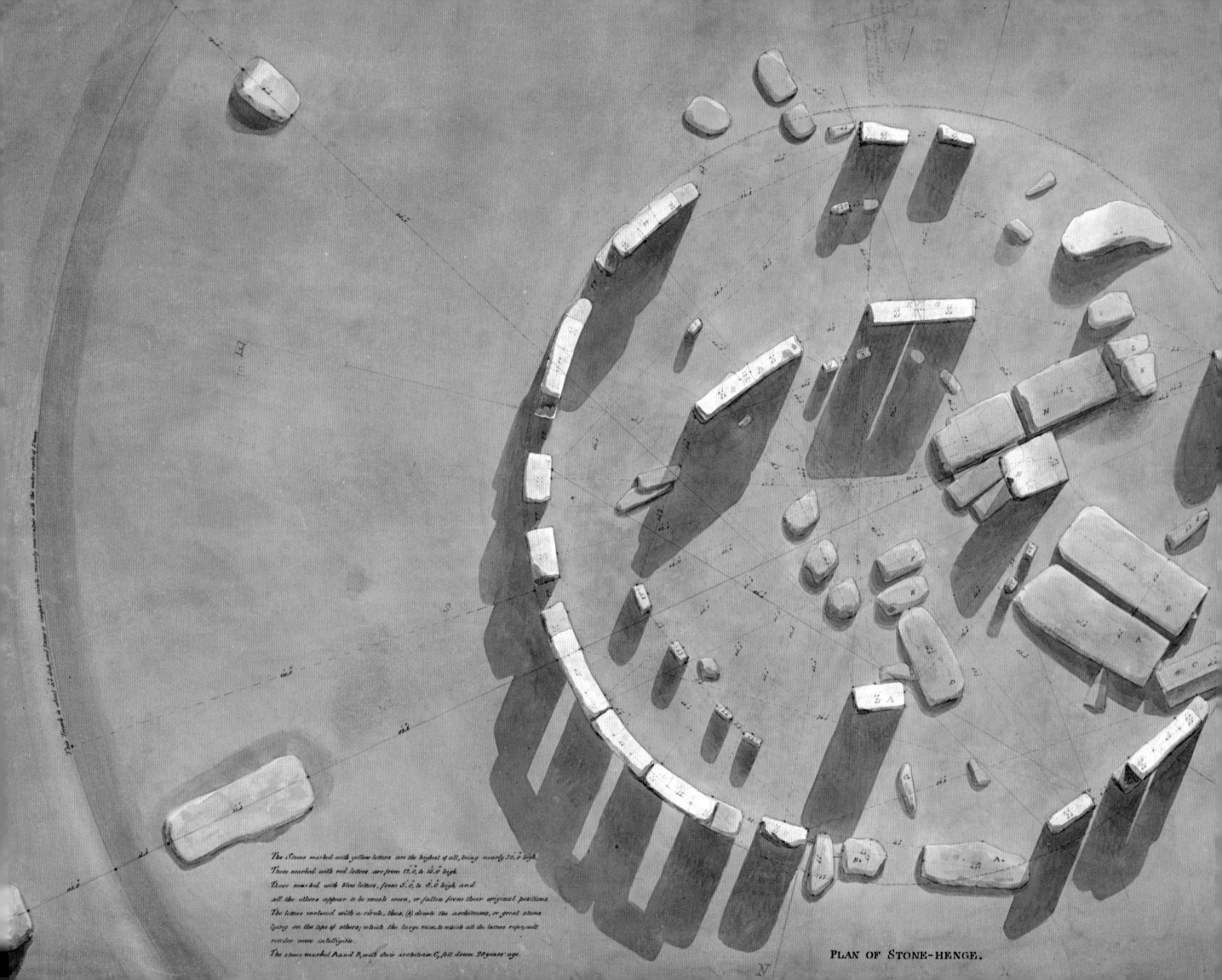

The Stones marked with yellow letters are the highest of all, being nearly 20.0 high.
Those marked with red letters are from 17.0 to 18.0 high.
Those marked with blue letters, from 5.0 to 8.0 high; and
all the others appear to be much worn, or fallen from their original positions.
The letters inclosed with a circle, thus, (A) denote the architraves, or great stones
lying on the tops of others; which the large ones, to which all the letters refer, will
render more intelligible.
The stones marked A and B, with their architrave C, fell down 20 years ago.

PLAN OF STONE-HENGE.

●— Henry Parke for Sir John Soane, RA lecture drawing, plan of Stonehenge, Wiltshire, 1817. SM 24/9/1. Photograph: Geremy Butler.

This plan is one of a series of seven lecture drawings illustrating Stonehenge and the druidical remains in the area, and it offers yet more proof of Soane's dedication to the education of young architects. From 17 June 1817 he sent three of his apprentices, George Bailey, Edward Foxhall junior (1793–1862) and Henry Parke, on a week-long journey to Wiltshire, which included a visit to Stonehenge on 21 June. The purpose of this doubtless costly excursion was two-fold: both as a means of exposing the young men to the architecture of that county, and in order to inform a series of lecture drawings, which were composed by Parke on his return to London. That Parke should be trusted with this task is unsurprising as he was Soane's second longest serving student, from 1814–20, and became an extremely talented draughtsman. In this drawing, not only is the arrangement of the stones shown with great care, but they are also coloured in order to delineate the larger stones that

remained standing. Moreover, lines are drawn onto the plan in order to offer an archaeo-astronomical explanation of their alignment. Soane was clearly interested in Stonehenge as he was in possession of first and second edition copies of Inigo Jones's *The most notable antiquity of Great Britain, vulgarly called Stone-Heng on Salisbury Plain* (1655 and 1725). Jones had been sent to survey Stonehenge by King James I and claimed that instead of being the work of the ancient Britons, it was instead a Roman temple dedicated to the sky god Coelus. Soane made no comment on this rather outlandish theory, but used two of Parke's Stonehenge drawings, including this plan, to illustrate his twelfth lecture, discussing architectural construction methods and the effort that must have been required to gather the blocks. 'The difficulty of constructing edifices of such astonishing grandeur and magnitude [as Stonehenge], the total disregard of expense where great national advantages were to be obtained so far beyond anything that modern times have produced, cannot fail to present themselves to the imagination of the artist.' (Sir John Soane, RA lecture 12.)

Sir John Soane's Museum

● — Joseph Michael Gandy for Sir John Soane, view of the Dome area at number 13 Lincoln's Inn Fields, London, 1811, SM 14/6/5. Photograph: Geremy Butler.

In 1807 Soane had acquired number 13 Lincoln's Inn Fields in order to expand the accomodation for his collection. Here the Dome area at the rear of the house is shown in perspective view, taken from a low vantage point so as to cleverly exaggerate the scale of the space. The most significant feature of the drawing is that the space is shown at night, with a powerful shaft of lamplight directed upwards from the Sepulchral Chamber below in order to illuminate – among other things – the life-sized cast of the entablature from the Temple of Castor and Pollux. Note that a figure can be seen in the shadows on the right-hand side, probably Soane himself, gesturing to the illuminated objects and inviting the gaze of the viewer. Of all the drawings showing Sir John Soane's Museum, this best explores the concept of *lumiére mystèrieuse* (mysterious light) that Soane so admired. It is a reminder of the various devices used by Soane in the building, such as top-lighting, floor grilles, coloured glass and mirrors, in order to create dramatic and emotive effects of light and shadow. Both the arrangement of the collection here and the cascades of light and shadow are reminiscent of the fantasy drawings of Giovanni Battista Piranesi, once again emphasizing the degree to which Soane had been inspired by his work. Previously misdated to 1813, the drawing was made for exhibition at the RA in 1811, but was also used later by Soane, in 1832, as an illustration to his sixth RA lecture.

●— **George Bailey for Sir John Soane, section through the Dome area at number 13 Lincoln's Inn Fields 'as it was in May 1810', London, 1811, SM 14/6/3. Photograph: Geremy Butler.**

This is another drawing depicting Soane's Dome area at number 13 Lincoln's Inn Fields, showing much the same arrangement and similarly illustrating an interesting time in the evolution of Soane's collection. Here we see a snapshot view of the arrangement in May 1810 of the objects within Soane's new Dome area at the back of number 13 – 'Various Architectural Subjects', as the inscription describes them – as well as giving detailed information on the architecture of the building itself. This reinforces the concept that Soane's house and collection functioned together as a single collective whole. Depicted in each bottom corner, there is a smaller drawing, unrolled as if for presentation: to the left there is a section looking east accompanied by miniature basement and ground-floor plans of the Dome area as they were at the time, and to the right there is an unbuilt design for the ground-floor plan of the entire building. This right-hand plan, showing an unbuilt design for the ground floor, is of particular interest as it illustrates Soane's intentions of 1809–11 for the building, with him living in number 12, and number 13 being taken over entirely by the collection. This concept was never realized, and instead Soane leased out the front, domestic portion of number 12, and created the domestic and museum spaces in number 13 that we know today. Note that the scene is dominated by the vast, life-sized cast of the entablature from the Temple of Castor and Pollux, which Soane so admired (see page 122).

This drawing was produced for the exhibition at the RA in 1811, both as a work of art in itself, and to illustrate Soane's evolving masterpiece at Lincoln's Inn Fields. The addition of clouds to either side of the main section is an example of a technique typical of presentation and exhibition drawings from the Soane office, offering greater interest than a basic orthogonal depiction while not distracting from the principal subject matter.

—•**Attributed to Joseph Michael Gandy for Sir John Soane, view of the principal façade of number 13 Lincoln's Inn Fields, London, late August 1812, SM 14/6/2. Photograph: Ole Woldbye.**
This crisply drawn view of the façade of 13 Lincoln's Inn Fields gives a design for the house which is close to how it was executed. Even now, number 13 is the most visible house in the northern terrace of Lincoln's Inn Fields as its stone façade contrasts with the flanking brick. Moreover, as can be seen here, it projects around 3ft (1m) in advance of the street frontage. The projecting stone portion of the façade was originally built as an open, balustraded loggia, but this was glazed in order to form extensions to the ground-, first- and second-storey rooms in 1829–34. The ornamentation seen here does survive *in situ*: most notably the incised mouldings and tablets of fret, which are typical of Soane's attenuated version of Neo-classical architecture. The figurative statues in this drawing represent a pair of Coade stone caryatids copied from the portico of the Erechtheum on the Acropolis in Athens (SM E6 and SM E7), which Soane purchased for £41 in November 1812. For those familiar with the Soane Museum, this drawing may appear rather spartan, and this is because Soane made additional embellishments to its façade. These include four Gothic corbels (actually the cap and shaft of statue pedestals) datable to the reign of Richard II, which are attached to the piers between the ground- and first-storey windows, and which had been recycled by Soane from the niches in the north front of Westminster Hall (SM E2–E4). Perhaps the most notable difference between this drawing and the building today is that it does not include the third storey, added in 1825, and originally containing the servants' quarters.

● Joseph Michael Gandy for Sir John Soane, view showing Soane's design for extending the façades of 13–15 Lincoln's Inn Fields, London, 1813, SM 74/4/1. Photograph: Geremy Butler.
Soane had purchased the freehold of number 13 Lincoln's Inn Fields in 1807 and subsequently rebuilt the house. This grandiose drawing depicts the façades of numbers 13, 14 and 15 as a matching group or urban palace frontage, indicating that Soane had at least considered the idea of purchasing further houses within the terrace. However, this is not a realistic conception as number 13 is not shown exactly as built, and it would be another decade before Soane purchased number 14, which he rebuilt to an alternative design. Moreover, number 15 never came into his possession. The drawing is perhaps a fantasy, but a rather charming detail can be seen in the inclusion of the figures of Soane and his wife Eliza on the first-floor balcony of the left-hand house. Additional information must be pieced together from various sources. We know that the drawing was exhibited at the RA in 1813, with the catalogue describing the drawing as 'Design for three houses, intended to form a centre, on the north side of Lincoln's Inn Fields, in part erected'. Further information can be found in an inventory of the collection by George Bailey, a one-time Soane office draughtsman and the first Curator of the museum. Bailey listed the drawing as 'view of a design for the façade of Three Houses in Lincoln's Inn Fields (13.14.15).' This confirms that the left-hand house is indeed number 13 and that the entirely fantastical design for the two neighbouring properties was proposed for numbers 14 and 15. Documents in the Soane Archive record that in 1813 two payments were made to Gandy of £50 on 30 January and £25 on 8 April (SM Archives Ledger D). These payments were for two drawings made for the RA exhibition of that year: this drawing and one of a design for the mausoleum at Dulwich Picture Gallery. This is by far the larger of the two drawings and would seem to account for the £50 payment making it datable to the very beginning of 1813.

Frank Copeland for Sir John Soane, section through the Dome area and the Breakfast Room at 13 Lincoln's Inn Fields, London, 10 June 1818, SM volume 83/1. Photograph: Geremy Butler.

This section by Soane's apprentice Frank Copeland (ND) cuts through the rear portion of number 13 Lincoln's Inn Fields from north to south. To the left we are shown the Dome area containing much of Soane's accumulated sculpture collection and to the right we can see his Breakfast Room. As such the drawing offers a succinct explanation of the dual purpose of the building, both as a home and a museum. The colouration of the drawing is particularly well applied and further demarcates the different areas of the building. The Breakfast Room is aglow, both from the colouration of its walls and from the painted and coloured glass within its lantern and top lights. Indeed, the Breakfast Room rightly deserved Soane's description as 'a succession of fanciful effects which constitute the poetry of architecture'. The basement Sepulchral Chamber and Crypt are shown in an emotive shadowy gloom as Soane always intended, while the Dome area is bathed in bright light from above, emphasizing the media of the plaster and stone objects contained within. The most commanding feature of the drawing is a cast of the Hadrianic-period marble Apollo Belvedere in the Vatican (SM M875). The cast of Apollo is seen here on the east side of the Dome area but was later moved to the west. From the mid-eighteenth century the Apollo Belvedere was considered to be the finest sculpture of antiquity and Soane had seen the original in Rome during his Grand Tour. This cast had been commissioned by the architect Richard Boyle, 3rd Earl of Burlington in *c.*1719. It later passed through other hands before arriving with Soane in 1811. Its installation at 13 Lincoln's Inn Fields was quite an undertaking, costing Soane £16.17.6½ to have the rear wall of the Dome area demolished, the cast created and then installed, and then finally to have the wall rebuilt.

The drawing is incorrectly inscribed '1817' on the recto, and on the verso it has the incomplete inscription 'F. Copeland June 10th 181[-].' Despite this, the drawing is datable to 1818 on account of the arrangement of objects in the Dome area, which includes items that Soane had purchased at the first sale of objects belonging to the Adam brothers in May 1818. Here is another drawing that offers an intriguing record of the evolution of Soane's collection and its arrangement within the museum.

—Joseph Michael Gandy for Sir John Soane, views of the Sepulchral Chamber and Picture Room at Sir John Soane's Museum, 9 September and 9 August 1825, SM volume 82/47, 90. Photographs: Geremy Butler.

Throughout the later decades of his life, Soane was careful in curating both his museum and also his legacy. It was doubtless in service to both of these that he commissioned numerous drawings of the museum and its contents. These two drawings of 1825 are found in a fascinating volume of *Sketches and Drawings of the House and Museum of J. Soane Esq RA* made between 1825 and 1836 and containing 125 drawings, the majority of them in the hand of either Joseph Michael Gandy or Charles James Richardson. These two drawings are typical examples from within the volume, being relatively small in scale, sketch-like but also meticulously accurate in their function as record drawings. The first gives a magnificent view from the basement level, from the Sepulchral Chamber looking east and up into the Dome area and with Soane's most expensive acquisition, the Sarcophagus of Pharaoh Seti I (SM M470), occupying much of the foreground. The other drawing shows Soane's Picture Room at the rear of number 14 Lincoln's Inn Fields, which he had created in 1824–5. In the centre of the room on an eighteenth-century ivory table (SM MGR2) there stands a 1770s cork model of the Temple of Vesta at Tivoli (SM MR2) in pride of place. However, the principal feature of the drawing is its depiction of the famous movable planes, and here we see those on the south side of the room, shown open to reveal a number of drawings illustrating Soane's own architecture. Here we see drawings within a drawing, hidden behind the Picture Room planes, and therefore this drawing illustrates Soane's most conspicuous 'hidden masterpieces'.

Joseph Michael Gandy for Sir John Soane, view of the Breakfast Room at number 12 Lincoln's Inn Fields, London, 1798, SM 14/6/1. Photograph: Geremy Butler.

Produced by Joseph Michael Gandy during his first year working as a draughtsman in Soane's office, this view is certainly attractive but does not demonstrate the unrivalled skill of Gandy's later work, and the human figures are comically out of scale. This was Soane's first Breakfast Room in Lincoln's Inn Fields, in his first house, number 12, built in 1792–4. It functioned both as an informal eating room and Soane's library. Bamboo chairs would have been understood at this date to indicate an informal environment, and the corresponding sixteenth-century Italian-style pergola ceiling was painted in 1793–4 by John Crace (1754–1819). Note that the pergola ceiling is painted onto Soane's earliest starfish vault, a motif which later became characteristic of his architecture. Here we see Soane, his wife Eliza and their then nine- and 12-year-old sons John and George, enjoying a moment of family repose, but equally we are given a sense of Soane's burgeoning status as a noteworthy collector, with five Piranesi engravings hung above the bookcases. On the right-hand side we can also see Soane's drawing of the Banqueting House on Whitehall for which he had been awarded the RA Silver Medal in 1772. The arrangement of the Breakfast Room seen here was lost when Soane moved into number 13 and took all of the furniture with him. The ceiling was gradually concealed under many layers of paint after Soane's death, but was uncovered again in 1969–70. A full restoration of the room was undertaken in the 1990s, offering an excellent example of the importance of architectural drawings to conservation and restoration projects.

Bibliography

R. and J. Adam, *The Works in Architecture of Robert and James Adam*, volumes I–III (1773–1822).

J.J.G. Alexander (ed.), *The Painted Page: Italian Renaissance Book Illumination: 1450–1550* (1995).

W. Aslet, 'A James Gibbs autobiography revisited', *The Georgian Group Journal* (2017).

S. Brindle, 'Royal Commissions' in S. Weber (ed.), *William Kent: Designing Georgian Britain* (2014).

I. Campbell, *The Paper Museum of Cassiano dal Pozzo: Ancient Roman Topography and Architecture*, volume I (2004).

Christie's, *A catalogue of a valuable library ... of the late Robert Adam, Esq. ...* (20–21 May 1818).

Christie's, *A catalogue of the collection ... of that eminent architect, John Nash, Esq. ...* (11 July 1835).

Christie's, *A catalogue of the genuine and valuable library and books, of the later Rt. Hon. C.F. Greville...* (2–3 April 1810).

Christie's, *A catalogue of the genuine and valuable prints and drawings, of that eminent architect, the late Sir William Chambers...* (6 June 1811).

Christie's, *A catalogue of ... the property of J. Paine, Esq. ...* (3 December 1830).

Christie's, *A catalogue of the whole and highly valuable collection ... of the late Joseph Nollekens, Esq. ...* (3–5 July 1823).

M. Collareta, '*Ciceronianismo e cristianesimo: Aspetti dell'arte sacra la tempo di Bembo*' in G. Beltramini et al., *Pietro Bembo e l'invenzione del Rinascimento* (2013).

H. Colvin, *A Biographical Dictionary of British Architects: 1600–1840* (2008).

G. Darley, 'Beginnings and early training' in M.A. Stevens and M. Richardson (eds), *John Soane Architect: Master of Space and Light* (1999).

G. Darley, 'The Grand Tour' in M.A. Stevens and M. Richardson (eds), *John Soane Architect: Master of Space and Light* (1999).

P. Davies and D. Hemsoll, *The Paper Museum of Cassiano dal Pozzo: Renaissance and Later Architecture and Ornament*, volume I (2013).

H. Dorey, *Catalogue of the drawings for Sir John Soane's Museum* (1990s, unpublished).

H. Dorey, 'Sir John Soane's "Union of Architecture, Sculpture and Painting" in his house museum in London' in M.T. Brandlhuber and M. Buhrs (eds), *In the Temple of the Self: The Artist's Residence as a Total Work of Art, Europe and America 1800–1948* (2013).

D. Esterley, *Grinling Gibbons and the Art of Carving* (1998).

L. Fairbairn, *Italian Renaissance Drawings from the Collection of Sir John Soane's Museum* (1998).

J. Fleming, *Robert Adam and his Circle* (1962).

S. Flood and T. Williamson (eds), *Humphrey Repton in Hertfordshire* (2018).

C. Fontana, *L'anfiteatro Flavio descritto e delineato dal cavaliere Carlo Fontana* (1725).

K. Garlick and A. MacIntyre (eds), *The Diary of Joseph Farington, Volume VI: April 1803–December 1804* (1979).

H. Hager, 'Carlo Fontana's project for a church in honour of the *Ecclesia Triumphans* in the Colosseum, Rome', *Journal of the Warburg and Courtauld Institutes*, XXXVI (1973).

E. Harris and N. Savage, *British Architectural Books and Writers: 1556–1785* (1990).

J. Harris, *Sir William Chambers: Knight of the Polar Star* (1970).

T. Knox, *Sir John Soane's Museum, London* (2013).

T. Kren and S. McKendrick (eds), *Illuminating the Renaissance: The Triumph of Flemish Manuscript Painting in Europe* (2003).

J. Lever, *Catalogue of the Drawings of George Dance the Younger (1741–1825) and of George Dance the Elder (1695–1768) from the collection of Sir John Soane's Museum* (2003).

J. Lever and M. Richardson, *The Art of the Architect* (1984).

B. Lukacher, *Joseph Gandy: An Architectural Visionary in Georgian England* (2006).

A. Matthews, '*A Great and Noble Design*': Sir James Thornhill's Painted Hall at Greenwich (2016).

R. Middleton, 'The History of John Soane's Designs for Public and Private Buildings', *The Burlington Magazine* (August 1996).

J. Musson, *In Pursuit of Antiquity: Drawings by the Giants of British Neo-Classicism* (2008).

J. Pinto, *The Trevi Fountain* (1986).

M. Postle (ed.), *Joshua Reynolds: The Creation of Celebrity* (2005).

M. Richardson (ed.), *Buildings in Progress: Soane's Views of Construction* (1995).

M. Richardson, 'Learning in the Soane office' in N. Bingham (ed.), *The Education of the Architect* (1991).

M. Richardson, 'John Soane and the Temple of Vesta at Tivoli', *Architectural History* (2003).

M. Richardson, 'Sir John Soane as a Collector of Drawings', Sir John Soane's Museum, *Soane: Connoisseur & Collector* (1995).

M. Richardson (ed.), *Soane: Connoisseur & Collector: A Selection of Drawings from Sir John Soane's Collection* (1995).

I. Roscoe, *A Biographical Dictionary of Sculptors in Britain: 1660–1851* (2009).

A. Rowan, *Vaulting Ambition. The Adam Brothers: Contractors to the Metropolis in the Reign of George III* (2007).

F. Sands, 'Grinling Gibbons as a master of two dimensions', Fairfax House Grinling Gibbons symposium paper (2018, unpublished).

F. Sands, '*Les dessins de chantier du bureau de John Soane*' in V. Nègre (ed.), *L'art du Chantier: Construire et Démolir du XVIe au XXIe Siècle* (2018).

F. Sands, *Robert Adam's London* (2016).

F. Sands, 'Sir William Chambers's forgotten masterpieces: a mausoleum for Frederick, Prince of Wales', Mausolea and Monuments Trust lecture (24 May 2018, unpublished).

F. Sands, 'The art of collaboration: Antonio Zucchi at Nostell Priory', *The Georgian Group Journal* (2011).

F. Sands, 'The Panic of 1772', T. Abrahams (ed.), *Year Zero* (2018–19).

F. Sands, 'Tracing the architecture of legacy: provenance, influence and Sir John Soane's drawings collection', Sir John Soane's Museum, *Death and Memory: Soane and the Architecture of Legacy*, (2016).

N. Savage, 'A Royal Academy student in architecture' in M.A. Stevens and M. Richardson (eds), *John Soane Architect: Master of Space and Light* (1999).

J. Shearman, 'Raphael, Rome and the Codex Escurialensis' in *Master Drawings*, volume 15, number 2 (1977).

J. Shearman, *Raphael's Cartoons in the Collection of Her Majesty the Queen and the Tapestries for the Sistine Chapel* (1972).

Sir John Soane's Museum, *A Complete Description of Sir John Soane's Museum* (2018).

Sir John Soane's Museum archives (reference numbers given in text).

Sir John Soane's Museum, online drawings catalogues: http://collections.soane.org/home (reference numbers given in text).

J. Soane, *A Description of the Residence of Sir John Soane, Architect* (1835).

J. Summerson, *The Book of Architecture of John Thorpe in Sir John Soane's Museum: The Fortieth Volume of the Walpole Society* (1966).

A.A. Tait, *The Adam Brothers in Rome: Drawings from the Grand Tour* (2008).

A.A. Tait, 'The Sale of Robert Adam's Drawings', *The Burlington Magazine* (July 1978).

The Champion newspaper, 24 September 1815.

The Holy Bible: King James Version: www.biblegateway.com

P. Thornton and H. Dorey, *A Miscellany of Objects from Sir John Soane's Museum* (1992).

P. Thornton, 'The Soane Gallery', Sir John Soane's Museum, *Soane: Connoisseur & Collector* (1995).

J. Turner (ed.), *The Dictionary of Art*, volume XXII (1996).

H. Walpole, *Anecdotes of Painting in England …* (1782).

G. Waterfield (ed.), *Soane and Death: The Tombs and Monuments of Sir John Soane* (1996).

D. Watkin, *Sir John Soane: Enlightenment Thought and the Royal Academy Lectures* (1996).

D. Watkin, 'Soane, Sir John (1753–1837), architect', *Oxford Dictionary of National Biography online* (2004–16).

D. Watkin, *Visions of World Architecture: John Soane's Royal Academy Lecture Illustrations* (2007).

J. Wilton-Ely, *Piranesi, Paestum & Soane* (2013).

Abmreviations

ARA	Associate of the Royal Academy
RA	Royal Academy/Royal Academician
RIBA	Royal Institute of British Architects
SAHGB	Society of Architectural Historians of Great Britain
SM	Soane Museum (used in reference numbers)

Index

Acknowledgements

O
ur knowledge of the drawings collection at Sir John Soane's Museum results from the accumulated research of forebears from throughout the nineteenth and twentieth centuries, not least that of former Soane Museum Curator Margaret Richardson who is a great authority on the subject of architectural drawings, and to whose work our understanding of the collection is much indebted. My gratitude is also due in no small degree to my current curatorial colleagues, Sue Palmer, Archivist and Head of Library Services, and Helen Dorey, Deputy Director and Inspectress, both of whom have assisted in the creation of this book, largely thanks to their decades of experience working with the Soane Museum collection and their unrivalled knowledge of its treasures. Other colleagues too have been heartily supportive and I am particularly grateful to Bruce Boucher, Deborah Loeb Brice Director, for his guidance and to Adam Thow, former Director of Commercial and Operations, for his role in negotiating all of the nuanced practicalities of publication that would never have occurred to my less pragmatic mind.

Many thanks are due to the Leon Levy Foundation, which very generously funded professional digital photography of the Soane Museum's entire drawings collection.

I would also like to thank those great scholars of drawings who have shaped my own knowledge and understanding of the subject, particularly Anthony Geraghty, Iain Gordon Brown, Gordon Higgott, Alistair Rowan and the late Jill Lever.

Finally, I would like to thank Batsford and Pavilion Books and its staff, particularly Lucy Smith, Tina Persaud and Lilly Phelan, for their enthusiasm and support for this project.

This book is dedicated to Rufus. I wrote it during your naptimes.

First published in the United Kingdom in 2021
by Batsford
43 Great Ormond Street
London WC1N 3HZ

An imprint of Pavilion Books Company Ltd

Copyright © B.T. Batsford Ltd, 2021
Text © Frances Sands, 2021
Images © Sir John Soane's Museum, 2021

ISBN: 9781849945851

A CIP catalogue record for this book is available from the British Library.

10 9 8 7 6 5 4 3 2 1

Reproduction by Rival Colour, UK
Printed and bound by Toppan Leefung Printing Ltd, China

This book can be ordered direct from the publisher at
www.pavilionbooks.com or try your local bookshop.

FSC MIX
Paper from responsible sources
FSC® C104723
www.fsc.org

© Granger Historical Picture Archive/ Alamy Stock Photo: p.20
© Heritage Image Partnership Ltd/ Alamy Stock Photo: p.21
© The Picture Art Collection/ Alamy Stock Photo: p.19
© National Galleries of Scotland/ V&A: p.20

—• Office of Sir John Soane, RA lecture drawing, montage of Sir William Chambers's various buildings at Kew Gardens, Richmond, 1806–19, SM 17/5/6. Photograph: Geremy Butler.